THE MAKING OF
ANDREY ZVYAGINTSEV'S FILM ELENA

CYGNNET

FILM-SCRIPT. OLEG NEGIN, ANDREY ZVYAGINTSEV	5
INTRODUCTION. OLEG NEGIN	51
THE DIRECTOR'S ANGLE. ANDREY ZVYAGINTSEV	57
CORRESPONDENCE WITH PRODUCER OLIVER DUNGEY	63
THE DIRECTOR'S PRODUCTION DIARY. ANDREY ZVYAGINTSEV	85
THE CAMERA'S GAZE. MIKHAIL KRICHMAN	135
THREE INTERVIEWS. QUESTIONS TO THE DIRECTOR	157

FILM-SCRIPT.
OLEG NEGIN, ANDREY ZVYAGINTSEV
(VERSION № 3 – NOVEMBER 14, 2009)

FILM-SCRIPT

1. EXT. VLADIMIR'S BLOCK OF FLATS. MORNING.
Early morning. The outside of Vladimir's flat. Through the dark trunks of trees a balcony is visible. The dim half-light gradually grows brighter. The air is filled with the first rays of the sun. Birds fly past the balcony, crows cawing in their usual way.

2. INT. VLADIMIR'S FLAT. MORNING.
A new day dawns. Kitchen, study, sitting room, part of the hall... The rooms are tastefully furnished. It is clear that the residents are far from poor.

3. INT. ELENA'S ROOM. MORNING.
Elena is sleeping in her bed. An electronic alarm-clock goes off. Elena immediately responds to it and turns it off. After waiting a short time, she sits up on the bed. For a short while she collects herself. Then she gets up from the bed, goes over to the small dressing-table by the mirror, sits down on the chair in front of it and begins to do her hair. She pulls it into a bun and brushes the rest. On the table there are two small group photos in frames. In the first Elena is wearing the white uniform and cap of a nurse, surrounded by several other people in white coats standing on steps in front of a hospital block. In the second there is a young couple in a registry office – a special, happy celebration (Elena's son Sergei and his wife Tatiana).

4. INT. SITTING ROOM/KITCHEN IN VLADIMIR'S FLAT. MORNING.
Elena draws the curtains in the sitting room and goes into the

ELENA. THE MAKING OF THE FILM

kitchen, turns on the television and prepares breakfast.

5. INT. SITTING ROOM/KITCHEN IN VLADIMIR'S FLAT. MORNING.
Elena opens the door into Vladimir's room and walks over to the window. She draws the curtains and light floods into the room. Elena walks past the bed, gently touches Vladimir's leg, as he lies sleeping under the blanket (in pyjamas).
Elena *(quietly)*. Good morning. Up you get.
She leaves the room. Vladimir briefly continues to lie there with his eyes closed (on his bedside table, apart from an alarm clock, there is a telephone in its cradle and a TV-remote. After throwing back the edge of the blanket, Vladimir begins to get up slowly, sitting for a while on the edge of the bed, facing the window and with his feet on the floor. At last he stands up and walks out of the room.

6. INT. SITTING ROOM IN VLADIMIR'S FLAT. MORNING.
Vladimir walks through the sitting room to the bathroom in his pyjamas and slippers. The bathroom door remains ajar. Vladimir washes himself. Elena comes out of the kitchen, walks past the bathroom and goes into Vladimir's room. It is visible through the open door that she is making the bed. Vladimir comes back into his room and they exchange greetings. When she has finished making the bed, Elena leaves the room and goes back into the kitchen. Vladimir takes off his pyjamas.

7. INT. KITCHEN IN VLADIMIR'S FLAT. MORNING.
Elena has prepared everything – the table is laid for breakfast for

FILM-SCRIPT

two. She is sitting on a chair at the table watching television and holding the remote. Vladimir comes in and Elena immediately turns off the television. She gets up, takes off her apron, folds it and hangs it over the back of a chair. Vladimir sits down at the table. Elena pours him a cup of coffee from a coffee-pot. Then she pours green tea for herself. She sits down at the table.
Elena. Enjoy your breakfast.
Vladimir. Thank you.
For a time they eat their breakfast in silence.
Vladimir. What are your plans for today?
Elena. I'm going to the bank to fetch my pension. Then I'm going to see Sergei.
Vladimir. Your Sergei ought to be coming round here. It's he who needs the money, not you. *(a pause while he chews)*. Why do you always drag yourself out there? Let him sort things out. He's a big boy now.
Elena. It's not just about money.
Vladimir. That's what you think.
He looks at Elena to make her aware of his empty cup.
Elena *(as she pours out more coffee)*. Let's not talk about it any more. I don't tell you how to behave with your daughter.
Vladimir *(taking a sip of coffee)*. All right, we'll leave it at that. I'll see you this evening. You're not going to stay the night there?
Elena. No.

8. INT. LANDING OUTSIDE THE FLAT. DAY-TIME.
Elena walks over to the lift and presses the button to call it.

9. INT/EXT. STREET OUTSIDE VLADIMIR'S BLOCK OF FLATS. DAY-TIME.
After coming out of the lift, Elena walks across the hall and goes out of the front door. A girl with a setter comes in through the entrance as she goes out. Elena walks along the pavement in front of the house, turns the corner and moves out of sight.

10. INT. BANK. DAY-TIME.
Standing by the bank counter, Elena counts her money and puts it away in her purse which she places in her handbag. She thanks the cashier and leaves the bank. The next person after her in the queue goes up to the counter.

11. INT. BUS. DAY-TIME.
Elena is riding in a bus, sitting by the window. There are raindrops on the window.

12. EXT. RAILWAY PLATFORM. DAY-TIME.
Elena approaches the station. A tram overtakes her. She walks up some steps leading to the station platform. A train pulls in. Elena comes out onto the platform and stops to wait for a train to arrive from the opposite direction.

13. INT. INSIDE THE SUBURBAN TRAIN. DAY-TIME.
Elena travels in an electric train, seated by the window.

14. EXT. SUBURB. DAY-TIME.
A suburban district consisting mainly of blocks of council flats. Elena walks along a path next to the concrete enclosure of an electricity sub-station towards some tall blocks of flats.

15. INT. SHOP. DAY-TIME.
Elena is standing by the check-out and the cashier hands her back her credit card. Elena packs her shopping into two plastic bags.

16. EXT. SHOP. DAY-TIME.
Elena leaves the shop with her plastic bags. At the corner of the building there is a cluster of stray dogs.

FILM-SCRIPT

17. EXT./INT. OUTSIDE/INSIDE SERGEI'S BLOCK OF FLATS. DAY-TIME.

Elena walks along the front of the block towards the entrance she needs. Three teenagers, sitting on a bench outside it, greet her. Elena walks in and then up some steps towards the lift. She calls the lift and waits. The walls near the door and the lift are covered with swear words, declarations of love, names of pop groups and gang graffiti...

18. EXT. VIEW FROM THE BALCONY OF SERGEI'S FLAT. DAY-TIME.

The beehive-like apartment block opposite Sergei's block of flats.

19. EXT. BALCONY OF SERGEI'S FLAT. DAY-TIME.

Leaning on the railing round his balcony and looking at the windows of the block opposite, Sergei (a man aged 36) is smoking. He spits on to the ground below.

20. INT. HALL OF SERGEI'S FLAT. DAY-TIME.

A small flat with two rooms and a kitchen. The doors leading into both rooms are open. In one of the rooms 17-year-old boy *(Sasha)* is playing with a PlayStation. Sergei is smoking on the balcony with his back to the door leading out onto it. The bell at the front door rings. Nobody hurries to open it. There is another ring of the bell. After a short pause a woman's voice *(Tatiana)* is heard from the kitchen.
Tatiana's voice. Is someone going to open the door?! Sasha!
Sasha grumpily tears himself away from his game and goes into the hall. He opens the door and Elena comes in carrying her bags of shopping.

Elena *(smiling at the boy)*. Hello, Sasha.
Sasha *(without managing a smile)*. Hi.
He is on the point of going back into the room with the PlayStation.
Elena. You can take these.
She hands him the plastic bags. With barely concealed irritation Sasha takes the plastic bags and moves off with them into the kitchen. Elena takes off her coat and shoes. Sergei comes into the hall.
Elena *(smiling)*. Hello, Sergei!
Sergei. Hi, Mum. In you come.
Without lingering in the hall, Sergei goes into the other room, where he sits down on the couch opposite the television, picks up the remote and switches on a comedy programme.

21. INT. ROOM IN SERGEI'S FLAT. DAY-TIME.
Elena comes into the room.
Sergei. Have a seat, Mum.
He pats the seat on the sofa next to him. Elena sits down and opens her handbag straightaway. She takes out the money and hands it to Sergei. He takes it, puts a few of the notes in the back pocket of his trousers and the rest – the bulk of it – into the pocket of his shirt. He gives his mother a quick kiss on the cheek and she strokes his head.
Sergei *(backing off)*. All right, all right.
A young woman holding a baby comes into the room. She and Elena greet each other. Elena gets up and with a radiant face stretches out her arms to the baby.
Elena. Let me hold him, Tatiana!
Tatiana hands the child to Elena.

Elena. Hello, my little one.
She gives him a hearty kiss on the cheek and hugs him.
Elena *(to her daughter-in-law)*. I've brought you money.
Tatiana. Thank you, Elena Anatolievna. As always, it's very well-timed.
Tatiana holds out her hand to Sergei with a demanding look. He takes the money out of his shirt pocket and hands it to his wife. She counts it and then walks over to the door to leave the room.
Elena. Tatiana, can you put the kettle on, please?
Tatiana nods and goes out of the room.

22. INT. HALL IN SERGEI'S FLAT. DAY-TIME.
As she comes into the hall, Tatiana notices that Sasha is putting on his shoes near the front door (he is holding some DVDs with computer-games).
Tatiana *(in a low voice)*. Where are you off to?
Sasha. I need to give some discs back to Viktor.
Tatiana. Your Viktor's not going anywhere. You can give them back later.
Sasha. I'll be back soon, Mum.
Tatiana. I know your 'soons'.
Sasha. He needs them in a hurry.
Tatiana. You and your Viktor are going to end up either in prison or doing military service. Is that clear?
Sasha. What's the point of me sitting round here like an idiot with you lot?
Tatiana. Well don't sit round like an idiot, sit round and use your brain! It's your future that's at stake. Or don't you care?
Sasha. All right then, all right.
Tatiana. Don't you just 'all-right' me. You'd be better off taking out the rubbish...
Sasha. In a minute.
Tatiana. We'll be having tea with Grandma soon.
Sasha goes off into his room, shutting the door behind him.

23. INT. KITCHEN IN SERGEI'S FLAT. DAY-TIME.
Elena, with the baby on her lap, and Sergei are sitting at the table in the small kitchen, while Tatiana, standing by the table, pours tea.

There is one extra cup because Sasha has slunk off into his room and still not re-emerged.
Tatiana. I don't know how to talk to him any more.
Sergei. I'll go and get him...
He gets up from the table and leaves the kitchen.

24. INT. CORRIDOR IN SERGEI'S FLAT. DAY-TIME.
Sergei goes to the door leading into the room with the balcony and with no further ado opens the door and stands on the threshold looking at Sasha, who is engrossed in his PlayStation game.

25. INT. ROOM WITH A BALCONY. DAY-TIME.
Sensing someone's presence in the room, Sasha looks over to the door.
Sasha. OK, I'm just coming, Dad! I just can't get on to the next level!
Sergei *(goes over to his son, looking at the screen with interest).* Give us a go...
He pushes Sasha over to one side, making the boy hand him the joystick.
Sasha. Dad!
Sergei. Give us a go, give us a go...
Reluctantly Sasha gives him the joystick. Sergei starts 'polishing off' the virtual villains.
Sergei. Watch and learn!

26. INT. KITCHEN IN SERGEI'S FLAT. DAY-TIME.
Tatiana and Elena, still holding the baby, are sitting silently at the table. It is clear that Tatiana is at her wits' end. Eventually she gets up from the table and goes out of the kitchen.

27. INT. HALL IN SERGEI'S FLAT. DAY-TIME.
When she reaches the open door leading from the balcony into Sasha's room, Tatiana stops on the threshold, looking at Sasha and Sergei.

28. INT. ROOM WITH A BALCONY. DAY-TIME.
Sensing his wife's presence Sergei looks round towards the door.
Sergei. We're just coming, Tatiana, just coming...
Tatiana looks at him in silence.

FILM-SCRIPT

Sergei. Tatiana, what's the matter with you? I'm talking to my son.
Tatiana. You'd be better off going to talk to your mother.

29. INT. KITCHEN IN SERGEI'S FLAT. DAY-TIME.
Elena, with the baby on her lap, Sergei, Tatiana and Sasha are sitting at the table in the kitchen and drinking tea. Tatiana directs Sergei's attention towards his mother, just by looking at him. Sergei nods.
Sergei. Well Mum, how are things going? Have you talked to him yet about Sasha?
Elena. Not yet, but I will, I will.
Sergei. Why are you dragging it out? We need to know in advance, whether we're going to have the money or not...
Elena. You know that Vladimir doesn't like requests like that very much. It's not that I've forgotten.
Sergei. He knows Sasha. They even seemed to be getting on all right. Are we relatives or not?
Elena. Vladimir is friends with everyone and no-one. You know... he's a law unto himself.
Sergei. He's just tight-fisted, your Vladimir, and that's all there is to it.
Elena. That's enough now, Sergei. If it wasn't for him, you wouldn't have what you've got now.
Sergei. And what have we got?
The question remains unanswered.
Sergei. Mum, we've got to help the lad avoid the army. It's best if we know straightaway: is he going to be able to be a student or has he got to go straight to bloody Ossetia. I'm right, Tatiana, aren't I?

(*turning to Sasha*) Sasha, what time's the football?
Sasha. Nine.
Tatiana (*turning to Elena*). Would you like some more tea, Elena Anatolievna?
Elena nods.
Tatiana (*as she pours tea into her cup*). We wouldn't keep troubling you so much, but you must realise that both in his school and the university we have to sort this all out with someone in advance. The 20th is the final deadline.
Elena. I get the picture. I'll talk to him, I will.

30. INT. VLADIMIR'S FLAT, VLADIMIR'S ROOM. EVENING.
Vladimir is lying on his bed on top of the bedspread watching a sports programme on the television (pole-vaulting).

31. INT. ELENA'S ROOM. EVENING.
The television is on ('Searching for Lost Friends and Relatives'). Sitting on her bed, Elena is writing something in a notebook resting on her knees. At a certain moment her attention is caught by emotional events in the programme and she looks up from her letter. After that she turns back to the notebook, completes what she was writing, tears out the page and leaves the room.

32. INT. SITTING ROOM IN VLADIMIR'S FLAT. EVENING.
Elena goes out of her room holding the letter and walks through the sitting room into Vladimir's room. She glances at him and notices that he has fallen asleep (he is already under the blanket, having turned the television off, but the lamp on his bedside table is still on). There is an open book lying on Vladimir's chest, which he had evidently been reading when he fell asleep. Elena goes into Vladimir's room, leaving the door open: she carefully picks up the book, closes it and places it on the bedside table. Hesitating as she does so, she places her note on top of the book, puts out the lamp and leaves the room. She closes the door and returns to her own room.

33. INT. SITTING ROOM IN VLADIMIR'S FLAT. DAY-TIME.
The door leading into Vladimir's room is open. Elena draws back the

FILM-SCRIPT

curtains – light floods into the room. Elena walks out of the room. Vladimir lies for a time with closed eyes, before finally pushing back the edge of his blanket and slowly sitting up. He remains sitting for a time on the edge of his bed with his feet on the floor. He catches sight of the note left on his bedside table the evening before by Elena. He picks it up and reads it.

34. INT. KITCHEN IN VLADIMIR'S FLAT. DAY-TIME.
Vladimir and Elena are finishing their breakfast. He is drinking coffee and she green tea.
Vladimir *(after a pause)*. I've read your note.
Elena says nothing.
Vladimir. So Sasha naturally will not be able to get in anywhere by the usual channels?
Elena. It's highly unlikely.
Vladimir. Why shouldn't he do his military service then? It's a good school for life.
Elena. But, Vladimir, you know what goes on in the army nowadays.
Vladimir *(after a pause)*. Tell me, why should I support your son's family? Why should I, all of a sudden, take on the burden of financing the studies of someone who, when all's said and done, is a stranger to me? I live with you, not with your relatives. You've known my view on this for a long time. Your Sergei has still not returned the money, which he borrowed from me three years ago, if you remember...
Elena. Yes, I remember. But you know the situation he's in at the moment.

Vladimir. I know your Sergei and his situation is perfectly clear to me. How many years has it been like that already? His whole life! I don't want to indulge him any more. If you like, you can call that a lesson.
Elena. You don't give lessons like that to your daughter... and never have done, I'm sure.
Vladimir. Elena, we're talking about your son at the moment. It's as if you don't hear what I'm saying. Let him try and apply his own mind to the problem. Let him get his backside off the couch and start doing something about it. If it was a question of the boy's health, God forbid, of course I wouldn't hesitate. The money would be on the table tomorrow.
Elena. It's precisely a question of his health. If you had a grandson, you definitely wouldn't let him serve in the army. *(her voice starts to shake).* Sasha needs help, that's all there is to it. To be given a chance...
Vladimir. Helping Sasha, helping Sasha! Elena, why do you bring the subject up. Leave my daughter out of it. I did everything I could for her and it's not my fault that she's turned out like her mother, who did nothing all her life, chasing pleasure all the time, and she's just another *(looks for a word)* hedonist.
Elena *(after a pause).* I don't know what that word means.
Vladimir. Selfish is what you'd say.
They do not say anything for a time, nor do they look at each other. Elena is the first to break the silence.
Elena. So can I count on you to help Sasha?
Vladimir. No you can't. I need to think about it. *(pause)* I hope you

are not taking money out of your account for them?
Elena *(after a pause).* If it's necessary, I can account for every rouble.
Vladimir. Why? There's no need for that. *(after a pause)* Forgive me, I got carried away. You know I have complete trust in you.
Elena does not say anything.
Vladimir. All right then. When is the money required?
Elena. The deadline's the 20th.
Vladimir. I'll give you an answer in a week. Let me have some more coffee.
Elena picks up the coffee-pot (from its weight she realises it's empty). She looks into it, picks it up and walks over to the work-top, where the coffee-maker is and pours coffee into the coffee-pot. Vladimir watches her. Elena comes back to the table and, standing by the table, pours coffee into Vladimir's cup.
Vladimir. What are your plans for today?
Elena. I'll be cleaning the flat.
Vladimir. Fine. I'm going to the gym.
Elena. I know.
Vladimir. I know that you know.
She goes back to her place. Vladimir picks up his cup, gulps down some coffee and takes a long look at Elena. Finally he stands up, takes her by the hand and leads her out of the kitchen.

35. INT. VLADIMIR'S ROOM. DAY-TIME.
Elena's blouse is unfastened and she is sitting on the edge of the unmade bed, tidying her hair. Vladimir's voice can be heard coming from the hall.
Vladimir. Elena, please bring me my sports kit.
Elena gets up from the bed, walks over to the wardrobe, opens it and takes out Vladimir's sports kit. Then she closes the wardrobe and leaves the room.

36. INT. HALL IN VLADIMIR'S FLAT. DAY-TIME.
Vladimir is putting the kit Elena brought him into his sports bag. After zipping the bag shut, Vladimir turns towards Elena and kisses her affectionately.

37. INT. LANDING. DAY-TIME.
Vladimir walks out of the flat with the sports bag over his shoulder and calls the lift.

38. INT. UNDERGROUND GARAGE. DAY-TIME.
After coming out of the lift Vladimir walks through the garage to his car. He gets into the driver's seat and puts his bag on the seat next to him. He turns on the engine and pulls away.

39. INT/EXT. VLADIMIR'S CAR/STREET NEAR HIS HOUSE. DAY-TIME.
Vladimir's car comes out of the garage and turns the corner. It stops at a pedestrian crossing and a straggling group of migrant workers crosses the street. After letting them pass, Vladimir drives on.

40. VLADIMIR'S CAR. DAY-TIME.
Vladimir drives through the town.

41. EXT. PARKING LOT AT THE FITNESS CENTRE. DAY-TIME.
Vladimir parks his car near the fitness centre.

42. INT. ENTRANCE HALL IN THE FITNESS CENTRE. DAY-TIME.
At the reception desk Vladimir exchanges his membership card for a locker key (there are two female staff in reception).
At the towel counter in the fitness centre a female attendant hands Vladimir a rolled up towel.

43. INT. CHANGING ROOM IN THE FITNESS CENTRE. DAY-TIME
Vladimir changes into his sports kit. He closes the locker and puts the key in his pocket, then leaves the changing room.

44. INT. TRAINING HALL. DAY-TIME.
Vladimir runs on the treadmill. It is noticeable that he has had a good work-out (he is sweating). He takes a closer look at a young woman working out on the 'pec-deck'. Their eyes meet, but then Vladimir looks away. When he comes off the treadmill he walks through the hall and stops by the water dispenser, takes a glass, fills it with water and drinks. The woman who had been on the 'pec-deck' walks past him from behind. Vladimir's gaze follows her.

45. INT. SWIMMING POOL. DAY-TIME.

Alone in the swimming pool, wearing a swimming cap and goggles, Vladimir enjoys swimming slowly to and fro using an amateurish breast-stroke. A female instructor wearing a track-suit is sitting on a chair in the corner of the room: she has backless sandals on her bare feet and is deeply engrossed in her women's magazine. Vladimir changes from breast-stroke to crawl and swims along with even, unhurried strokes, but suddenly the strokes stop and his arm flops heavily into the water. He stops moving, face downwards in the water, like a large white fish stunned with dynamite. The instructor does not notice what is happening at first, but once she does she calls to Vladimir:
Instructor. Hey...hey!
On receiving no answer, she throws down her magazine, gets up and jumps into the water without taking off her track-suit.

46. INT. VLADIMIR'S FLAT. KITCHEN. DAY-TIME.

Elena pays the delivery-man who has brought in her food shopping, standing at the kitchen table. He gives Elena her change. The carrier-bags with food are on the table and the receipt next to them. After shutting the door behind the delivery-man, Elena goes into Vladimir's study taking the receipt and money (small change) with her.

47. INT. VLADIMIR'S STUDY. DAY-TIME.

After unlocking a small safe using a code (the safe is built into one of the side sections of Vladimir's desk) Elena places the money in it and the receipt (there are several bundles of money of various currencies in the safe – roubles, dollars, euros).

48. INT. KITCHEN. DAY-TIME.

Elena comes back into the kitchen, puts the food away in the fridge. The telephone rings. She picks up the receiver.
Elena. Hello... Yes, it's me.

49. INT. HOSPITAL WARD – LUXURY CLASS. DAY-TIME.

Vladimir is lying on a hospital bed with closed eyes under a drip. Two small oxygen tubes have been inserted into his nose. A nurse is standing next to the bed. She is adjusting the flow in the drip.

Elena comes in with a white coat thrown round her shoulders. She nods to the nurse, who nods back. After adjusting the drip, the nurse leaves. Elena sits down on a chair next to the bed. She looks at Vladimir. As if he has sensed her gaze, he opens his eyes and turns his head towards her. For a while they look at each other in silence.
Vladimir *(speaking slowly and with some difficulty)*. D'you remember? This was how we met.
Elena. Of course.
She leans forward and takes hold of his hand.
Vladimir. What year was it?
Elena. It'll be ten years ago in December.
Vladimir. I'd give anything not to be here as I am now, but to be back there then. Appendicitis – however bad – is still better than a heart attack.
Elena. That appendicitis wasn't much better. Or rather peritonitis, to be exact.
Vladimir *(with a sad laugh)*. You medic, you. Of course it was better. If for nothing else than the fact that you were working in the hospital then. Although the girls here aren't bad either.
Elena. If you go on like that I'll cut off your oxygen. Then you'll know what's hit you!
Vladimir. You might well do it! Have you spoken to the doctor?
Elena. Not yet.
Vladimir. All he does is reassure me, saying they won't be keeping me here for long.
Elena. So things aren't too bad then?
Vladimir. Or the very opposite.

FILM-SCRIPT

Two doctors come into the ward – a man and a woman (the woman is holding Vladimir's care plan and would appear to be the doctor on his case: the man is the head of department).
Head of Department *(turning to Elena)*. Could you leave us on our own for a little while?
Elena gets up from her chair and walks over to the double-door.
Vladimir. Elena, please ring Katerina.
Elena nods. The doctors sit down on the chairs by the bed: the head of department on the chair Elena was using and the other doctor on the other side of the bed.

50. INT. HOSPITAL CORRIDOR. DAY-TIME.

On her way out of the ward Elena can no longer hold back her tears. She takes a handkerchief out of her handbag, presses it to her eyes and walks over to the window at the end of the corridor. After wiping away her tears and standing by the window, she makes a call on her mobile phone.

51. KATERINA'S FLAT. DAY-TIME.

Katerina (a young woman aged about 30) is sleeping on a bed. A mobile phone rings. Katerina opens her eyes.
Katerina *(calling to someone in the next room)*. Give me my phone please.
A young man, sitting at a table in front of a computer, picks up the receiver which, till then, has been lying on the table and takes it to Katerina. After taking the phone, Katerina presses a key and lifts it to her ear.
Elena's voice in the receiver. Hello Katerina. It's Elena.
Katerina. Yes, hello.

52. INT. HOSPITAL CORRIDOR. DAY-TIME.

Elena is still standing by the window.
Elena. I'm sorry but I have bad news for you. Your father's in hospital. He's had a heart attack. He wants to see you. I hope you'll come over.
Katerina's voice in the receiver *(after a pause)*. I can't today. I'll come tomorrow.
Elena. Well, all right then. But before that I'd like to meet you for

a brief chat.
Katerina's voice in the receiver. Is that really necessary?
Elena. Yes, I think it is.
Katerina's voice in the receiver. All right then, where?
Elena. Wherever's convenient for you.

53. KATERINA'S FLAT. DAY-TIME.
Katerina is lying in bed, talking on her phone.
Katerina. It's you that's asking, you suggest somewhere.
Elena's voice in the receiver. All right. Not far from here I noticed a small café.
Katerina. Where is that?
Elena's voice in the receiver. Write this down.
Katerina. I'll remember it.
She gets up from the bed and walks into the other room with her phone at her ear. When she comes up to the table at which the young man is sitting in front of a computer, Katerina – now that the conversation with Elena is over – puts her phone down on the table, kisses the young man and sits down next to him at the table. Both of them look at the screen.
The opening shots of the film *Žižek!* appear: Slavoj Žižek is shown in close-up (we hear his first remark and the voice of his interpreter, when Katerina has already come into the room. Later on, while Žižek goes on speaking, we are shown Katerina and the young man all the time).
Žižek. What would be my – how shall I call it – spontaneous attitude towards the Universe? It's a very dark one. The first thesis would be a kind of total vanity – there is nothing... I mean it quite literally. Ultimately there are just some fragments, some vanishing things. If you look at the Universe – it's one big void. But then how do things emerge? Here I feel a kind of spontaneous affinity with quantum physics. Where the idea is that the Universe is a void, but a positively charged void. And then particular things appear when the balance of the void is disturbed. I like the idea of spontaneity very much. The fact is that there isn't just nothing. Things are out there. It means that something went terribly wrong. What we call Creation is a cosmic imbalance. A cosmic catastrophe. Things exist by mistake. And I am even ready to go to the end and to claim that

FILM-SCRIPT

the only way to counteract it is to assume the mistake and go to the end. We have a name for this, it's called 'Love'. Isn't love precisely a cosmic imbalance? I was always disgusted with these notions such as "I love the world", "the Universe is love". I don't like the world, I don't know... I'm basically somewhere in between "I hate the world" or "I'm indifferent towards it". But the whole of reality is just it. It is stupid. It is out there. I don't care about it. Love for me is an extremely violent act. Love is not "I love you all". Love means – "I pick out something" – it's like a structure of imbalance – even if that something is just a small detail. A fragile individual person, I say "I love you more than anything else". In this quite formal sense, Love is Evil.

54. INT. CHURCH. DAY-TIME
Elena walks into the open door of a church. Inside it might as well be empty – in one corner near the entrance there is a woman wearing a headscarf sitting by a box of candles. After standing and hesitating by the entrance, Elena looks from side to side and then walks over to her.
Elena. Good morning.
Woman with a headscarf. Good morning.
Elena. Could you advise me?..
Woman with a headscarf. Would you please cover your head?
Suddenly remembering what is required, Elena brings a scarf out of her handbag and ties it round her head.
Elena. I wanted to ask you... Where should I place my candle?
Woman with a headscarf. For a sick person or someone who's died?

Elena. You see, my husband's in hospital...
Woman with a headscarf. Then you need a 'get-better' candle. Write your husband's name down on a piece of paper so that the priest mentions him in his prayer for the sick and you must place a candle in front of St. Nicholas and the Mother of God. When you place your candle, ask the Lord to make him better and to help him.
Elena buys candles from her.
Elena. Excuse me, but where are those icons you mentioned?
Woman with a headscarf. Straight down and you'll see them to the right of the altar.
After going up to an icon, Elena places the candle before it. At first she has difficulty lighting it. All she does is make the wax melt and then, at last, she manages to light it properly...

55. INT. CAFÉ. DAY-TIME

Elena is sitting in a half-empty café at a table with a cup of tea.
Katerina comes in. Elena beckons her over.
Katerina walks over to the table and sits down.
Katerina. Hello, Elena Anatolievna.
Elena. Hello, Katerina. Do you want to order something?
Katerina. I'll make do.
She takes out a crumpled packet of cigarettes from the back pocket of her jeans and starts smoking. She looks straight at Elena, who looks away as she takes a sip of her tea.
Elena. What I wanted to say was that your father has had a heart attack...
Katerina. I get it.

Elena. He's very weak.
Katerina. But conscious at least...?
Elena. Yes, he's conscious, thank goodness.
Katerina. He's probably groped all the carers by now.
Elena. Katerina!
Katerina. Yes, Elena Anatolievna...
Elena. I want to ask you to be gentler with him. It's very important for him to get proper rest. Katerina, he needs all the love you can give him. Show him that you love him.
Katerina says nothing, while looking straight at Elena.
Elena. You see each other rarely as it is, which I don't understand at all, but that of course is your business.
Katerina. Precisely.
Elena. You never telephone him. It shouldn't be like that. I even think that this attack...
Katerina. But of course, it's all the prodigal daughter's fault...
Elena. To some extent, I do think that...
Katerina. Listen a moment, Elena Anatolievna, I'm well aware that you're playing the role of the caring wife. You've got it down to a T, well done. But that's enough. Let's call it a day.
Elena. I love Vladimir.
Katerina. Oh yes, till death do you part. I don't doubt it. Like a true medic, Elena Anatolievna, you're trying to cure me, but I'm healthy and don't need curing. What I've grown into, that's over and done with.
Elena. Don't you feel sorry for your father?
Katerina. I realise that's a rhetorical question. Nevertheless, I'll

still give you an answer. I don't give a flying fuck.
Elena. Oh Lord...
Katerina puts out her cigarette.
Katerina. Which ward is he in?
Elena. Katerina, just listen a moment... I think it'd be better if you didn't see him today. Put it off for a bit, when he's feeling stronger.
Katerina. Where's the logic? Why did you ring me yesterday then? You should have rung when he was feeling stronger.
Elena. Your father asked me to.
Katerina. Which ward is Papa in?

56. INT. HOSPITAL WARD. DAY-TIME.
Katerina is standing by the window with her back to it. She's leaning against the edge of the window sill and looking at Vladimir. He is looking at her at the same time.
Vladimir. I can hardly see you, Katerina.
Katerina. That's because I'm standing against the light.
Vladimir. I didn't mean that.
Katerina. There's no meaning anywhere, Papa.
Vladimir. Looking at you that's what I think sometimes as well.
Katerina. So it's a good thing you can hardly see me.
Katerina moves away from the window, sits down on a chair after first moving it further away from the bed and crosses her legs.
Katerina. I've never been the meaning of your life. And thank goodness as they say!
Vladimir. You're wrong there.
Katerina. Money, Papa. It's always only been money that gave your

life meaning.
Vladimir. You sound as if you're settling scores. Money's important to you as well.
Katerina. Not to the same extent.
Vladimir. That's because you've never earned any yourself.
Katerina. And that's because you spoiled me too much and pandered to my every whim.
Vladimir. That sounds like criticism.
Katerina. Heaven forbid, Papa – I worship you. Please continue in the same vein.
Vladimir. I don't understand why I do it.
Katerina. You don't understand what you're paying for?
Vladimir. What I'm being made to pay for...
Katerina. But not in tears, all right?
Vladimir. You just love playing with words...
Katerina. Through play is how a child learns the stern laws of reality.
Vladimir. Are you thinking about a child?
Katerina. No. I haven't been and I won't be. Don't worry, I'm not pregnant, if that's what you're thinking.
Vladimir. Pity. That would calm you down.
Katerina. Alcohol and drugs – only at weekends... That's how I'm living at the moment. Sex and food are the only pleasures I don't seem able to ration. But I'm working on it. You can be sure of that.
Katerina takes a packet of cigarettes out of her pocket.
Vladimir. What on earth... are you going to start smoking here?
Katerina. Why not. After all, you've paid for this luxury suite. You

can do whatever you like.
Vladimir. Katerina, this is a hospital.
Katerina. So?
Vladimir. You must be joking?
Katerina. OK, then, I'll go and smoke where I'm allowed to.
She gets up from her chair.
Vladimir. Wait a bit.
Katerina. Well, what is it?
Vladimir. Where do you get all that hate from?
Katerina. Where do you think? Genes, Papa, it's hereditary. Rotten seeds. We're all rotten seeds. Sub-human...
Vladimir. Give birth and bring up some better ones. Give it a go, you'll make a good job of it.
Katerina. There haven't been any 'better' ones and there never will be. I have no particular urge to experiment in that field. It's painful and expensive. And there's no point.
Vladimir. What is it about you? For you everything's pointless. It's an idiotic excuse. All you want to do is run away from responsibility.
Katerina. What's irresponsible, Papa, is producing children who you know in advance are going to be ill and doomed, because the parents – to put it mildly – are already ill and doomed, doing that merely because everyone else is doing it, as if there's allegedly some higher meaning attached, which we, alas, are not destined to find out, since we are merely instruments of an unfathomable higher will. Shit must be tasty because millions of flies can't have all got it wrong. When all's said and done the world's coming to an end soon

— in case you didn't know.
They look at each other for a long time.
Vladimir. However strange it might sound, when listening to you, I feel a good deal better.
Katerina. That's why you keep multiplying — sucking energy from your own offspring and then you ask in surprise: "Where do you get all that hate from?"
Vladimir. What a little fool you are, Katerina!
Katerina. Thank you.
Vladimir. I love you so much.
He holds out his rather shaky hand to her.
Katerina *(despite herself, she creases up her forehead)*. Let's get by without all of that, OK? *(She puts her cigarettes away in her pocket)*. I'll smoke later. I don't feel like it any more.
Lingering as she makes ready to leave, Katerina takes Vladimir's hand.
Katerina. What people won't do for money!
Vladimir *(he laughs)*. You see, you're starting to understand things, you're finding some meaning.
Katerina. The important thing is that you shouldn't lose it.
Vladimir. Parasite!
Katerina. Really? I was told you'd had a heart attack!
Vladimir *(he laughs and pulls her over towards him)*. Let me give you a kiss.
Katerina. So the patient appears to be alive rather than dead!
She bends over towards her father, giving him her cheek to kiss.

57. INT. HOSPITAL WARD. NIGHT.

Vladimir is watching television. A documentary film about a plague of locusts is being broadcast. With some difficulty, Vladimir raises himself to a sitting position, lets his feet down on to the floor and sits like that for a time. Then, holding on to the edge of the bed with a rather unsteady hand, he stands up slowly and heads off to the door leading out of the ward.

58. INT. HOPSITAL WARD. DAY-TIME.

Lying in bed Vladimir is talking to a man in a suit and tie and wearing glasses *(a lawyer)*. A nurse comes in (the men break off their conversation). She greets them, looks at the care plan, leaves the ward and walks off down the corridor.

59. INT. HOSPITAL CORRIDOR. DAY-TIME.
Vladimir is being discharged. Elena pushes Vladimir's wheel-chair out of the ward. Apart from her, the head of department, Vladimir's other doctor and a nurse are present.
Head of department. For quite a long time it will be important to keep to a strict time-table for his medication without mixing anything up. Keeping to the diet is essential as well.
Elena nods.
Head of department. I would recommend that you take on a properly qualified carer.
Elena. I myself looked after patients in a professional capacity for many years. I worked in a hospital.
Head of department. In that case, that's fine. I wish you all the best then. You can always reach me on my mobile.

60. INT. VLADIMIR'S FLAT. VLADIMIR'S ROOM. EVENING.
Evening. Vladimir is lying in his bed in the bedroom and holding the TV-remote: a football match is on.

61. INT. ELENA'S ROOM. EVENING.
In her room Elena is sitting on her bed and watching television (a programme on topical new trends). The programme comes to an end and Elena turns off the TV.

62. INT. VLADIMIR'S ROOM. EVENING.
Evening. Elena goes out of her room and walks towards Vladimir's. His door is slightly ajar and the sound of the television can be heard (the football is still on). Elena goes into Vladimir's room. He is sleeping with the remote still in his hand. She carefully takes away the remote, turns off the television, straightens Vladimir's blanket, turns out the bedside lamp and leaves the room. She leaves the door slightly open and goes back into her own room, the door of which she also leaves ajar.

63. INT. VLADIMIR'S ROOM. DAY-TIME.
Morning. On a special over-bed tray in front of Vladimir, who is

lying in bed, can be seen the remains of an invalid's breakfast and a small plastic beaker containing tablets. Elena is sitting on a chair next to the bed and holding a cup of green tea on a saucer. Vladimir takes his pills, tipping them all into his mouth without even looking into the beaker. On the bedside table there is an electronic device for measuring blood pressure.
Vladimir. Elena, I need to tell you something.
Elena. I'm listening.
Vladimir *(pause)*. It's strange that I hadn't done it before... As if I'd been planning to live forever...
Elena says nothing and looks into her cup.
Vladimir. Well. There's no point in beating about the bush. To cut a long story short, I've decided to write a will.
Elena. Forgive me, but I'm not comfortable listening to this.
Vladimir. No, Elena, it's important. I feel I have to be honest with you. Everybody's time comes. Let's call a spade a spade. When all's said and done, we think about these things, whether we like it or not.
Elena. No, that's not true.
Vladimir. Nevertheless I think we have to have this conversation.
Elena. It's up to you.
Vladimir *(after a pause)*. Apart from you and my daughter I don't have any other relatives... After my death Katerina will receive virtually everything. You, as my wife and loyal companion of my twilight years, will receive an annuity. It will be paid to you every month and you can be assured that you will not want for anything. They look at each other for a long time, each taking in the implications of what has just been said.

Vladimir. That's all. I'd been preparing to tell you all this for a long time and blurted it all out in a mere ten seconds. I can see you want to say something.
Elena. It doesn't have anything to do with what you were saying, but as I see it this is as good a moment as any and I should like...
Vladimir. Go on, out with it.
Elena. It's the business... that business with Sasha...
Vladimir *(frowning)*. Oh, yes, Sasha... I've thought about that too, I've been mulling it over. This is what I think, Elena. It seems to me that his father, your son, must see to all of that.
Elena. But Vladimir...
Vladimir. What were they thinking about when they had him? And then they went on to have another one.
Elena. It was an accident.
Vladimir. Both times? Don't make me laugh.
Elena. I don't see anything funny here. It just happened and that's all there is to it. It could happen to anyone.
Vladimir. Precisely, it could happen to anyone. But the point is, Elena, it doesn't just happen, they do it themselves. And they ought to take responsibility. Without hoping a kind uncle will come along.
Elena shakes her head, clearly intending to say something, but then thinks better of it.
Vladimir. Elena, I don't begrudge them the money. You must understand...
She suddenly interrupts him in an aggressive tone, which seems out of character.
Elena. Of course not, since you're giving it all to your foolhardy daughter.
Vladimir. For a start, not all of it. And secondly, you don't know much about her – she's extremely rational.
Elena. She's foolhardy and off the rails.
Vladimir. That's enough now.
Elena. And infertile apparently.
Vladimir. Don't be ridiculous. She's just... different. Not like you and I.
Elena. Are you trying to say she's not like my son and his children?
Vladimir. It's you that said it.
They look at each other challengingly, but then Elena looks away

FILM-SCRIPT

and lowers her head. They sit like that for a time: Vladimir thinking his thoughts with a commanding air and Elena thinking hers in dismay.

Vladimir. I have been responsible with regard to Katerina and she, I hope, will find a way...

Elena *(quietly, without raising her head)*. What right do you have?

Vladimir. What d'you mean?

Elena. What right do you have to think that you're special? Why? Just because you've got more money? More possessions? That could all change.

She raises her head and looks at Vladimir.

Vladimir. What precisely could change, Elena?

Elena. "And the last shall be first."

Vladimir. Hmm. Well and what will they do with those who were the first before them? Surely you don't think they'll share out the newly won benefits? I doubt it. What I mean is I do not imagine they're all going to live in 'equality and fraternity.' If such a thing were possible at all, then surely only somewhere in your Kingdom of Heaven... That's all just a bible story, isn't it? Just fairy-tales for the poor. Elena, are you listening to me?

Elena nods her head, not really looking at Vladimir but through him into the middle distance, thinking some thought of her own, which has suddenly occurred to her.

Vladimir. Let's leave it at that. You've probably got plenty of things to do.

Elena gets up and takes away the tray with the remains of the breakfast.

Elena. Do you want anything else?
Vladimir. I want you to understand me properly.
Elena. I do.
Vladimir. Elena, we must get all this out of the way.
Elena. We shall.
Vladimir. I think so too. I'm glad that you've understood me. Please bring me a pen and paper. I'm going to do a draft version of my will. In a few days I'll need to call my lawyer round.

64. INT. KITCHEN IN VLADIMIR'S FLAT. DAY-TIME.

Elena loads crockery into the dish-washer. She closes it, but does not switch it on. She stands next to it for a while, leaning against the worktop. Then she walks out of the kitchen.

65. INT. VLADIMIR'S STUDY/VLADIMIR'S BEDROOM. DAY-TIME.

Standing by the desk Elena picks up some sheets of paper (about 20) and a pen and then she goes from the study into Vladimir's room and hands him the pen and paper without saying anything. Vladimir gives her a nod by way of thanks. She leaves his room in the direction of her own.

66. INT. ELENA'S ROOM. DAY-TIME.

Elena makes a telephone call standing by the window.
Elena. Hello, Sergei... All right, thank you... Vladimir? He's better but still weak. *(pause)*. Listen... we've talked about Sasha. *(pause)*. I'm afraid we're going to have to cope on our own... Yes, that's how it is... He thinks that you as the father need to sort out the problem...

Just stop... That's enough, I beg you! I'm very upset myself! But... I do think – don't get me wrong – that there is some truth in what he says... We'll sort things out. I don't see any other way... We'll think of something... Yes, I'll ring again later.

67. INT. KITCHEN IN SERGEI'S FLAT. DAY-TIME.
Sitting at the kitchen table, Sergei puts down the phone.
Sergei. Damn it, tight-fisted old devil!
Calming down he gets up and opens the fridge taking a long look into it.
Sergei *(calling loudly towards the other rooms)*. Tatiana, where's my beer?
Tatiana *(from the next-door room)*. Have you been to fetch the baby milk?
Sergei. There was a bottle of beer in here!

68. INT. ELENA'S ROOM. DAY-TIME.
Elena sits for a long time on her bed, deep in thought.

69. INT. SITTING ROOM/STUDY IN VLADIMIR'S FLAT. DAY-TIME.
After leaving her room Elena walks through the sitting room into the study. She goes over to the bookshelves and looks for a particular book there, which she finds. It is a pharmaceutical reference book.

70. INT. KITCHEN IN VLADIMIR'S FLAT. DAY-TIME.
Elena settles down at the kitchen table and slowly leafs through the reference book. Every now and then she lingers over a particular page. Finally she finds what she is looking for and reads one page carefully.

71. INT. BATHROOM IN VLADIMIR'S FLAT. DAY-TIME.
When she comes into the bathroom, Elena opens the bathroom cabinet containing her and Vladimir's toiletries and medicines. She looks for something among the medicines and finally lights upon it. It is a packet of 'Viagra'. Elena takes a long look at it, opens it, takes out the tablets and instructions (one of the four tablets has already been used). She reads the instructions and then, still holding the packet, shuts the cabinet and leaves the bathroom.

72. INT. KITCHEN IN VLADIMIR'S FLAT. DAY-TIME.
Elena is making a special lunch for Vladimir: she washes fruit and vegetables, chops up some lettuce in a food-processor, switches on a juice-extractor and prepares juice.
After preparing Vladimir's meal and placing it on the over-bed tray laid out on the kitchen table, Elena puts out his pills in the plastic beaker. After hesitating a moment she then adds two 'Viagra' tablets to the beaker, placing them under the rest.

73. INT. VLADIMIR'S ROOM. DAY-TIME.
Some screwed up sheets of paper covered with writing are lying round the bed. The rest of the paper – smooth empty sheets – is on the bedside table with the pen, next to the telephone. Vladimir is holding the TV-remote and watching the sports channel (football). Elena comes in holding the over-bed tray.
Elena. What a mess you've been making!
Vladimir. I just can't concentrate. Nothing's turning out right.
He puts the TV-remote down. Elena arranges the lunch tray in front of him. Vladimir picks up a fork.
Elena. Pills first.
Vladimir. All right, all right.
Without looking at the pills he empties the beaker into his mouth, washes them down and begins to eat. Elena leaves the room and shuts the door behind her.

74. INT. KITCHEN IN VLADIMIR'S FLAT. DAY-TIME.
After leaving Vladimir's room, Elena goes into the kitchen and sits down at the kitchen table.

75. INT. VLADIMIR'S ROOM. DAY-TIME.
Vladimir has finished eating. He drinks the glass of juice while watching the television (football).
Vladimir. Elena!
A few seconds later Elena comes into the room.
Vladimir. I've finished. Thank you.
Elena. Are you going to have a rest now?
Vladimir. Yes, I'll sleep for a bit.
He picks up the TV-remote and switches off the television. Elena

goes over to the window and draws the curtains. Then she goes back to Vladimir, picks up the cordless phone from its cradle on the bedside table and places it on the over-bed tray with the remains of the lunch. She picks up the tray and leaves the room.

76. INT. KITCHEN IN VLADIMIR'S FLAT. DAY-TIME.

After returning to the kitchen, Elena clears the remains of food from the plates and arranges them in the dish-washer. She takes a tablet from a box on a shelf and places it in the machine, which she then switches on. She leaves the kitchen.

77. INT. ELENA'S ROOM. DAY-TIME.

Back in her room Elena sits down in her usual place on the bed. After sitting there for a while, she lies down with her face to the wall, shading her eyes with her hand and with her knees bent up. She lies there for a long time. All of a sudden, as if she has heard something, Elena draws her hand back from her face, turns her head towards the door and after listening hard, finally gets up and goes into the bathroom, where she turns on a tap. After a while it can be heard how she turns off the tap and goes back into her room. She comes out hesitantly.

78. INT. SITTING ROOM IN VLADIMIR'S FLAT. DAY-TIME.

Elena slowly approaches Vladimir's room, stops by the door and listens, but there is not a sound to be heard from inside.

79. INT. VLADIMIR'S ROOM. DAY-TIME.

Elena opens the door slightly ands peers into the room. She sees Vladimir silently shaking with convulsions on the bed – his face is grey, his eyes bulging and the veins on his neck swollen. It is clear that he cannot breathe. Elena, paralysed with fear, freezes in the doorway: she is unable to tear her gaze away from the sight, which 'fortunately' does not last very long. Vladimir exhales and then crumples; his head drops back onto the pillow. Elena's knees are giving way underneath her: she puts her hand out to the wall to stop herself falling over and gently sinks to the floor. Her whole body is trembling and she shuts the door with a feverish movement.

80. INT. SITTING ROOM IN VLADIMIR'S FLAT. DAY-TIME.

Elena is sitting on the floor by the door into Vladimir's room. Her back is against the wall. She sits like that for a long time, shaking all over. Eventually she makes an effort to collect herself, turns towards the door which leads into Vladimir's room, opens it a crack and at the same time slowly pulls herself upright.

81. INT. VLADIMIR'S ROOM. DAY-TIME.

Vladimir is lying motionless in the same pose. Only the whites of his eyes are visible. His mouth is open and one arm is hanging down limply by the side of the bed.
As she stands in the doorway Elena takes a long time to summon up the courage to cross the threshold: eventually she goes in and walks over to Vladimir. More in control of herself by now, she bends down, lifts his arm and feels his wrist for his pulse. Without letting go of his arm, she feels for Vladimir's pulse on his neck as well. Then she pulls back his eyelids. After making sure he is dead, she feverishly collects up the discarded drafts of his will, still lying on the floor by the bed, straightens out the sheets of paper and then gets down on her knees to make sure that none of the pages has slipped under the bed. There is nothing there.

82. INT. KITCHEN IN VLADIMIR'S FLAT. DAY-TIME.

Elena comes into the kitchen with the sheets of paper, straightens them out, briefly scanning the incomplete will and then she burns them in a Pyrex saucepan, which she places on one of the hotplates. She switches on the extractor and washes away the ash down the sink, before thoroughly washing the saucepan. Then she picks up the cordless telephone and leaves the kitchen.

83. INT. VLADIMIR'S ROOM. DAY-TIME.

On entering the room, Elena makes sure once again that Vladimir has no pulse. Then she tidies the blanket over him, looks carefully round the room and places the telephone on the bedside table next to the packet of 'Viagra'. After that she goes out into the corridor.

84. INT. SITTING ROOM IN VLADIMIR'S FLAT. DAY-TIME.

As she walks slowly into the kitchen, Elena dials a telephone number to call an ambulance. She waits for an answer.

85. INT. SITTING ROOM IN VLADIMIR'S FLAT. DAY-TIME.

The ambulance-service doctor is sitting on a sofa by the coffee-table in the sitting room, writing his report on the call-out. He certifies Vladimir's death, on the table in front of him lies an empty packet of 'Viagra'. Elena looks rather cowed as she sits next to the doctor on the sofa. In Vladimir's room two medical orderlies are placing the body in a plastic sack.

Doctor *(as he finishes his report he looks up).* I can't believe it. Surely they must have warned you that he shouldn't be having sex at the moment. Pills like that are quite out of the question.
Elena. I didn't even know that he had them.
Doctor. It's really childish behaviour, I have to say. Plenty of mindless teenagers would have had more sense.
Elena. You might be a little more tactful.
Doctor. I've been a model of restraint.

86. INT. CREMATORIUM. DAY-TIME.

Funeral hall. Quiet music is playing. An expensive open coffin containing Vladimir's body has been laid out on a stand in the middle of the hall and at a slight distance from the coffin there are several rows of chairs.

Elena dressed all in black (her eyes are blood-shot and she is holding a handkerchief), is sitting in the front row and on the chair next to her friend (the woman seen in the group photograph on the table by the mirror in Elena's room). Behind them, in the second

and third rows, are several other people (among them the man who had visited Vladimir in hospital – the lawyer – and also a general with his wife. Almost all those present are more or less the same age as Vladimir). Katerina comes into the hall wearing dark glasses. She goes over to the coffin and eventually bends down and kisses her father's forehead and then moves away from the coffin. She does not go over to Elena but sits down at some distance from her.

87. INT. VLADIMIR'S FLAT. ELENA'S ROOM. MORNING.

Morning. Elena is lying on her bed and has clearly only just woken up. She is looking in an absent fashion out of the window. At last she gets up, walks over to the dressing-table, sits down on the chair in front of it and brushes her hair.

88. INT. KATERINA'S FLAT. MORNING.

Morning. A young man is asleep in the room on the bed *(Katerina's boyfriend)*. Katerina is sitting with her feet up on the sofa and there are tears in her eyes. The young man wakes up and when he finds Katerina is not next to him, he looks round and catches sight of her. He gets up and goes over to her and for a while stands there in silence.
Young man. D'you want some tea?
She nods and the young man goes into the kitchen. Katerina remains alone.

89. INT. VLADIMIR'S FLAT, VLADIMIR'S ROOM. MORNING.

Morning. The curtains are drawn. Sunlight is coming in through the crack between them. Elena is standing by the window, looking out

pensively. Eventually she draws back the curtains and light floods into the room. Elena turns round and leaves the room. Vladimir's bed has now been made up tidily.

90. INT. KITCHEN IN VLADIMIR'S FLAT. MORNING.

Elena is having breakfast (she looks rather different from the way she did during breakfast with Vladimir. She is not untidy but somehow more casual. She has no make-up on and her hair has not been brushed, just pinned back any old how. She is not wearing a plain dress as before but has put a dressing gown on over her nightdress). The television is on.

91. INT. STUDY IN VLADIMIR'S FLAT. DAY-TIME.

(Elena is now clearly making ready to leave the house: she is tidily dressed in an austere outfit). After kneeling down in front of the desk, Elena opens the safe and takes out money from it (there is nothing else in the safe). She closes it, gets up, puts the money into a large envelope which she had made ready in advance and then puts the packet into her bag. She zips it shut and leaves the room.

92. HALL IN VLADIMIR'S FLAT. DAY-TIME.

Elena puts on her coat and looks at her reflection in the mirror. She goes back into the sitting room and sits down on the edge of the sofa. She sits there for a long time, her eyes downcast.
The telephone rings. Elena picks up the receiver, which has previously been lying on the coffee-table.
Elena. Hello, yes...

93. INT. LANDING IN THE BLOCK OF FLATS. DAY-TIME.
After locking the door of the flat (she rattles her keys as she puts them away in her handbag), Elena goes over to the door of the lift and presses the button to call it.

94. INT/EXT. ENTRANCE TO VLADIMIR'S BLOCK AND THE STREET OUTSIDE IT. DAY-TIME.
After coming out of the lift, Elena goes out of the block of flats and gets into a taxi, which has been waiting for her at the entrance. The taxi moves off and turns at the corner of the building.

95. INT. INSIDE THE TAXI. DAY-TIME.
Sitting on the back seat of the car and holding her bag on her knees, Elena travels along the streets of the city.

96. INT. LAWYER'S OFFICE. DAY-TIME.
Elena (holding her bag on her lap) and Katerina are sitting in armchairs in the lawyer's office. He is sitting opposite them at his desk and looking through some papers. His secretary comes in with a tray – coffee for the lawyer and green tea for Elena. She places a drink in front of each person and then leaves the office. The lawyer looks up from the papers and peers over his expensively-framed glasses at Elena and Katerina.
Lawyer. Well, Vladimir Ivanovich appears to have sensed he was soon to die. As his lawyer I know how he wished to dispose of his property. I visited him in hospital at his request. We discussed the subject.
The lawyer pauses for a moment, looking first at one woman and then the other.
Lawyer. Unfortunately we had not put his wishes in writing, as is required by law. As a result I am bound to state the following...
He pauses again.
Lawyer. Vladimir Ivanovich did not leave a will and the principle of legal succession comes into force. Firstly I wish to inform you that he did not leave any debts. Otherwise, after receiving your inheritance you would have had to assume responsibility for satisfying his creditors. I am also bound to inform you that, according to the law *(he continues looking every now and then at the text of the law)*, should

one spouse die, the surviving spouse has the right to a portion of any jointly acquired property during the period of their marriage, i.e. to their share of the conjugal property. In addition the surviving spouse, on an equal basis with other heirs, inherits the deceased spouse's share of that (jointly acquired) property, which forms part of the inheritance together with property which had been the personal property of the deceased.

Katerina takes out her cigarettes. The lawyer passes her an ashtray.

Lawyer. In this case, however, circumstances took shape in such a way that in the two years, during which you, Elena Anatolievna, were officially married to Vladimir Ivanovich, you did not acquire any joint property. So no reference need be made to any spouse's share. Like Vladimir Ivanovich's daughter Katerina, you Elena Anatolievna, will inherit part of the deceased's property. In other words – so as to keep it simple – since there are no other heirs, as far as I know, all the inheritance will be shared out between you in two equal parts. *(pause).* If that is not clear or you have any questions, I am happy to explain anything as required.

Katerina *(addressing the lawyer).* I know that my father always kept a considerable amount of cash in his safe at home. What will become of that?

Elena *(speaking before the lawyer has a chance to say anything).* I have already checked and there is nothing there. It would seem that...

Katerina. That's all clear then. The question can be dropped.

Elena. You must believe me, Katerina.

Katerina. Let's leave it at that then. *(she turns to the lawyer).* What else?

97. INT. SUBURBAN ELECTRIC TRAIN. EVENING.

Evening. Clutching the handbag on her lap tightly, Elena is travelling in an electric train, sitting by the window. Suddenly the train 'shudders' and begins to slow down with an unpleasant scraping of the rails. The train stops. It stands still for a long time. A squad of policemen walks quickly through the carriage. People are getting worried.

At last the electric train moves off again. People start looking curiously out of the window – first to one side and then the other. They are trying to see what had caused the unscheduled stop and

the long wait. Soon the reason is clear (on Elena's side of the train). At a level-crossing slightly to one side of the track there lies a bleeding horse, its legs still shuddering. Some people are looking at it, unable to do anything about it. Not far away there is an overturned springless carriage, to which the horse must have been harnessed. The train gathers speed. Elena clutches her handbag tighter than ever.

98. EXT. SUBURB. EVENING.

Dusk gathers. Elena walks quickly past the five-storey houses of the suburb. When she reaches the house, where her son lives, she disappears into the entrance.

99. INT. SERGEI'S FLAT. KITCHEN. EVENING.

The lights are on. There is a large bundle of foreign currency on the kitchen table next to Elena's open handbag. Standing round the table and looking at the money without saying anything are Elena, her son Sergei, his wife Tatiana holding the baby and Sasha.
Elena *(addressing Sergei).* Well, my lad, everything should turn out differently for us now.
Sergei. We need to celebrate this.
Nobody objects. Sergei leaves the kitchen and soon comes back with an open bottle of cheap cognac and three glasses. He puts the glasses down on the table and pours 100 grams into each of them.
Tatiana sits down on a chair and settles the baby on her lap. Elena sits down as well. They raise their glasses.
Sergei. To Vladimir! At least he's done one good deed in his life.

Elena. No. Let's drink to Sasha.
Tatiana. For his new life.
Sergei. Yes, and Mum! We've got a surprise for you, you know *(he keeps her guessing)*. We're expecting again!
Elena. Really? God, that's wonderful!
Tatiana. For a new life!
Sergei. If it's a boy, we'll call him Vladimir.
Elena *(turning pale)*. I really hope that... that it'll be a girl.
Sergei. It would be good! Let's drink to that!
They start drinking: Elena and Tatiana take a sip, Sergei downs his glass in one. He then pours himself another glass straightaway.
Tatiana. Slowly does it.
Sergei. We can drink today. Relax, don't spoil the party. What a great day!
He downs another glass. Suddenly the lights go out in the kitchen and everything is in total darkness. It is almost impossible to make out faces or the shapes of objects. The only light comes from the dim street.
Elena *(in a frightened voice)*. What was that?
Sasha *(in otherworldly voice)*. Game over.
Elena grabs at Sergei's arm in genuine fear.
Sergei. Ma, what's got into you? It's just the circuit-breaker. It happens every now and then. You'll be tearing my arm off soon. Let go.
But Elena cannot let go. She needs to hold on to something. Sergei pulls her arm away from his.

100. INT. SERGEI'S FLAT. CORRIDOR. NIGHT.

Stretching out his arms in front of him, Sergei walks through the dark space towards the front door of the flat, feels for the lock and opens the door. Outside it everything is pitch black.
Sergei. Well I never, it's not just a fuse. Look, it's the whole block! The whole world! – *(a loud voice echoes from higher up the stairs and it is followed by guffaws and screeches in the hoarse voices of some teenagers and the clinking of bottles...)*
Sergei. To hell with them...
The whole district seems to have lost power *(a calm man's voice is heard to one side of them).*
Sergei. Alexei Vasilievich, is that you?
He peers into the darkness and steps out onto the landing.

101. INT. LANDING IN THE BLOCK OF FLATS. NIGHT.

A face appears on screen in profile and lit from underneath by the quivering tongues of a candle flame. A man is standing in front of an open switchboard, peering into it with a puzzled expression.
Alexei Vasilievich. They'll probably switch everything back on again soon.
He shuts the switchboard cover.
Sergei. Bloody wretches, that's the second time in a month.
Electricity suddenly comes back on.
Hurrah! – *(the youths in the stairwell shout out and clink their beer bottles)* – The end of the world is over!
Sergei and Alexei Vasilievich nod at each other and then go back to their respective flats. All that can be seen in the shot after that is the electricity meter: the disc is turning and the numbers are moving.

102. INT. CHURCH. EVENING.

Holding an unlit candle Elena goes up to the table of remembrance. Standing in front of the table on which there are many burning candles (the table is 'crowned' with a rectangular candle-holder, to which a gilded crucifix has been attached), Elena puts down her candle 'for the departed'. She lowers her eyes and stands by the table for a long time. Finally she turns round and moves towards the exit. In the meantime a lay brother has come up to the table of remembrance and started blowing out the candles one after the other.

103. EXT. NEAR THE CHURCH. EVENING.
Elena comes out of the church, walks away from it and stops by a smart car (we recognise it as Vladimir's), opens it and sits down in the driver's seat. While she is switching on the engine, another car stops nearby in the same parking lot and a priest wearing a dark coat over his cassock gets out: he is talking on his mobile phone and carrying a briefcase in his free hand.
Priest. Yes, yes, my dear... I'm happy to hear you too... OK, we're getting along all right, thank the Lord... What about you?..
Meanwhile Elena's car moves slowly off.

104. INT. CHURCH. EVENING.
On the table of remembrance there are still some burning candles. The lay brother is blowing them out and collecting them up.
The priest is putting his mobile phone away in his briefcase as he comes into the church. He disappears through a door. In the meantime the lay brother is completing his duties. A watchman crosses himself as he comes into the church: after putting out all the candles he and the lay brother turn off the lights and lock all the doors. They shut the main door from the outside and everything falls quiet.
Some dim light is still coming into the church from outside the windows. Some icon lamps are still gleaming. Complete silence reigns and the peace of night, as it draws in, grows ever more intense in this frightening space.
The altar looms ever darker in this grim and all-pervading 'isolation'.

THE END

The film was shot according to the 4th edit of the film-script. The main difference from the text published here is in the three final episodes (102/103/104), which significantly differ from the film. We decided to include this earlier version of the text to show the creation process of the final film-script.

INTRODUCTION. OLEG NEGIN

INTRODUCTION

> If therefore the light that is in thee be darkness,
> how great is that darkness!
> *Matthew 6:23*

While animals may kill out of necessity, as they say – as part of the food chain, they rarely kill a relative, and more rarely still eat a relative – a bear that eats other bears is a rare occurrence. On the other hand, man kills in his search for gratification – more often than not for assumed advantage to himself, but on occasion for the actual act of taking life.

Elena's acknowledgement to Vladimir, that she does not understand the meaning of the word 'hedonist', appears to demonstrate her natural purity of heart – she is not seeking gratification: she is acting out of necessity.

This is a false lead, which the audience unconsciously follows, inexorably drawn to the conclusion, that what stands before them is an animal, a beast. What they are actually confronted by is a Human Being.

An unconscious search for gratification is the only thing that propels Elena forward (as indeed all the other characters). There is no doubt that she will achieve her aim. At any cost.

People of widely differing levels of intellect and possessing varying quantities of human warmth have said after seeing the film *Elena*:

INTRODUCTION

"It's about me... " and that's the plain truth.
The vast majority of them have said: "It's a frightening film. Horrifying!" That too is true.

It is one thing to be able to look in a mirror and deceive oneself with a flattering angle or pleasant perspective. It is another to confront yourself in the darkness of the cinema, just as you are or as you will soon no longer be.

Here the only deception is that you have been invited to participate in what would seem a familiar procedure – to look at yourself in a mirror: "Yes there are weak points, but in general I'll pass muster! Especially if I turn this way, or that..!" – but you have been shown not a reflection, but reality.

Very few recognised the Beauty of the image before them (although virtually everyone was impressed by it). More's the pity. Those who did recognise it, found themselves happily laughing. The play of light and shade, once discerned, can tickle us to death. Yet the sharp-eyed among us are able to pull back from the edge.

At the 'social level' the characters I personally find fascinating are Vladimir – all-powerful, a symbol of corrupt and increasingly decrepit political power; Elena – a mother figure, a 'Russian soul' with an enduring strength that extends beyond the ordinary world; Katerina who embodies young, yet barren democracy lives for the present in every sense of the word, including the very absence of sense itself; Elena's children who stand for the people – the very source of power.

Elena is beautiful. Divinely so. As a mother figure, epitomising the Great Goddess, her actions are perfectly executed. Clever film-goers will laugh, those who are less sharp will be left puzzled. All around her is *Kali-yuga*[1] – moral degradation... Truthfulness is the only virtue which we can appreciate in the world of today. Purity, Self-denial and Compassion are slumbering. All the intellectual veneer – morality, principles and dignity – are elusive, only recent acquisitions.

---

[1] Kali-yuga – according to Hindus the 'Dark Age' of spiritual degradation.

In a purely action-based scenario this fine varnish is instantly blown away – when 'necessity calls', then our basic instinct (the search for gratification – meaning), which has evolved over tens or hundreds of thousands of years of human existence, takes centre stage – as large as life, blocking out everybody and everything else: genes, heredity...

Some people prefer to devour their neighbours alive. Protests from the victim only excite the devourer. This is referred to by that all-powerful word 'survival'. One person will go all out to survive at the expense of another and when access to that source is closed off, he will simply remove him from life altogether.

Surely all this is amusing? Walking about in glasses, shoes and a coat, expressing ideas, playing the piano, writing poems, prancing around, wearing all sorts of crosses and amulets, building churches and mansions, composing songs about love, compassion and luxury, brandishing moral values and principles by the ton – in both hard-cover and paperback versions – believing in a higher purpose, climbing on to a pedestal of virtue and saintliness, dabbling in erudition, teaching children what is good and kind and enduring while, to all intents and purposes is remaining an incorrigible beast of the very worst kind – a Human Being merciless as he lunges hungrily towards just one thing – gratification.

The pinnacle of creation...

Moo!

In India people do not eat beef. In Russia, on the other hand they say (almost harking back to Sanskrit): "If you lose the rope, you'll lose the cow" or "My cow's died, let the neighbour's die too".

For *Elena* to be born, my father had to die (a man of the most honest principles).

I just gathered the nectar. Like a bee. Immortalised it as honey. In my own way. As best I could. Thank you Papa, your life was not in vain.

THE DIRECTOR'S ANGLE. ANDREY ZVYAGINTSEV

THE DIRECTOR'S ANGLE[1]

In his innermost self every person is strikingly alone. Loneliness is the beginning and end of human lives, a red thread that runs right through them.

Throughout this project I have been fascinated by the chance to look into an idea central to our times: survival, saving oneself at any cost. Both disconnection from those around us and individualism are leading mankind to a point where we shall be no better than spiders trapped in a glass jar. In step with the growth of individual freedoms for society there has to be parallel growth in solidarity.

We see before us people in late middle age in a relationship that appears perfectly normal. We might even say that these people love each other, although not with the heady love of youth. Their gentle care and tact, combined with a firm sense of what is just, serve to convince us that love has brought them together for all time. Yet even if the word 'love' can be used to designate any form of negotiated relations between two individuals, when moments of crisis befall such relations, each will opt for him or herself.

Concepts of humane behaviour are being devalued before our very eyes and at ever increasing speed. In this situation the individual becomes more and more immersed in himself, reverting to ancient instincts and his animal origins.

---

[1] This document dates from August 2009.

The female praying mantis devours the male during the very act of mating. She is interested in only one thing – the survival of the species, her instinct to reproduce.

This will be a pitiless, uncompromising look at human nature: a hard, up-to-the-minute drama filmed in the language of today. As for its form or its movement in time, our future film appears to me as a fast-moving, tense tightening of a spring round the main event – the heroine's decision to kill. While until that point in the film, we have been shown a tender and caring woman, filled with gentle devotion, in the culmination of the drama we see before us a monster, whom we can scarcely recognise any more. From that moment the rapid pace slows down and, in the short space of time left before the end of the film, time will move as if it were a human being caught up in ordinary day-to-day preoccupations, who has grasped the mechanistic and meaningless nature of the events taking place around him.

A monster in the shape of a fine upstanding person standing like a repentant sinner before their idols in a church – surely that might be an image for the end of time?

The Devil is powerless in the face of God. Man is powerless in the face of Death and God is powerless in the face of human choice... The future of that triangle is only to be found in the hands of Man himself.

THE SEVEN LETTERS.
CORRESPONDENCE WITH PRODUCER OLIVER DUNGEY

THE SEVEN LETTERS.
CORRESPONDENCE WITH PRODUCER OLIVER DUNGEY

1. First Letter

I like the core of the story – very much in fact: I think the ideas are rich for exploration and the plot could make for an intense and tightly bound story – but I do think the plot needs some work. At this stage, regardless of the direction in which you want to take this film, I feel we should concentrate on the mechanics of the plot, on its structure. Naturally, any amendments depend a great deal on what you hope to achieve with this story. I happily make that your responsibility. Nevertheless, I have put some comments below; they are fairly general and I hope they encourage you and Oleg to develop and enrich the plot as you see fit.

As I see it, the story contains themes of great potential – the responsibility of parenthood, the sins of our fathers affecting the lives of our children, the abuse of power and the corruption of wealth, the fight between nature and nurture, the compulsion of love, the intrinsic goodness within human beings etc. – and the characters can be built up into great complexity and humanity. I have no doubt that, with work, a film of very high quality can be fashioned from these elements.

I would also like to suggest placing the film in a specific time and place, a time and a place that has an appeal in and of itself. Perhaps you might like the idea of setting the story against the backdrop of political unrest or some form of rebellion, a time when a country or a community are undergoing a shift in power (after the abuse of power?). An obvious example would be the end of colonial times; alternatively, you might imagine a situation from the near and recognisable future. There might be places in the world that intrigue you enough to set your story there. I leave that thought with you.

As I said, I think the plot needs some work; which is another way of saying that the interrelationships between the characters need some work which, in turn, suggests that the characters themselves need some work. I think they need building up.

Below I have put a few of my impressions about Helen and Richard[2]. I then go on to make a series of more general points, not especially well-ordered, but I hope they might prove useful to you in some way.

Helen:
I understand the importance of Helen's meekness but, as I read it, I feel that she has also been denied the qualities of competence and maturity. And I believe that this is causing problems with the story.

I think she has the potential to be an admirable individual and I would like to see her invested with a little more competence and charisma – after all, she used to work in a hospital. Could she be imbued with the qualities of a matron? She could be sensible, well-ordered, no-nonsense, competent in the little aspects of life (and thus quite capable of arranging a death – can we foreshadow her actions by showing she has the capacity for them?) but without flair and without an eye for the bigger picture. And because she lacks flair and an eye for the bigger picture, she has found herself in her situation – dependent on a man for the happiness and prosperity of her family. She could be a woman of love and great competence who is a victim of circumstance.

As I read it, however, she seems a little infantile (a cousin to meekness): she has an ambivalent attitude to figures of authority; she makes no attempt to resolve her situation herself – like a child, she hopes the figure of authority will just fix it; she is overcome with child-like fear during the power cut; and her attitude to life seems a touch unsophisticated, certainly compared to Richard's. And in this simplicity there lies both two-dimensionality and a certain amount of delusion; I see this in the way she does not have fully engaged

---

[2] The first version of the script contained English characters: Helen (Elena), Richard (Vladimir), Catherine (Katerina), Dan (Sergei) and Henry (Sasha).

relationships with those in her family: her marriage is strangely stunted, she ignores the reality of her son, she pays no attention to her daughter-in-law, she is viewed without affection by her grandson. She does not seem to engage with the truth of the people around her. Conversely, Richard does engage with his daughter and he seems to see the reality of the world more clearly.

Of course, I may have misunderstood your intentions – her meekness and, for want of a better word, her immaturity might be the very qualities that draw you to this story. "Blessed are the meek for they shall inherit the earth." In which case, I think her character fits awkwardly into the plot – she does, after all, murder her husband. Perhaps the answer is to understand her better. Or perhaps the answer is to think of the plot as Richard's tragedy but seen from the viewpoint of Helen, a secondary character in his tragedy but the main figure in the film? [...]

In short, I am worried that there will be little affection for Helen as she is at the moment. But the structure of the plot implies that we should have affection for her. Ultimately, if we are to share her hopes, should she not provoke a little more admiration – and therefore identification – and a little less pity? There seems to be a fracture between the plot and the character.

Richard:
At this stage it is my inclination to build up the characters – and their interrelationships – especially so if the characters are the embodiment of certain philosophical ideas – if they are, in essence, mythological. I would suggest working up the characters, and working up their story, and then paring the plot down to only what is essential within it.

Richard is the most interesting character to me at the moment – for example, he is the only character that needs to reconcile two contradictory emotions: this is seen mostly clearly in the scene with Catherine – confronted with the reality of family relationships, Richard adopts the same approach as Helen and has his own arguments used against him.

He has his ideas about the world; he is cynical and, most probably, worldly and experienced. In comparison to Helen, this makes him seductive.

However, Richard is without focus. He thwarts Helen but he seems to have no desires otherwise. What is he doing with himself? At the moment, he is passive – he is neither trying to achieve anything nor is he trying to protect himself in any way.

Can we see Richard as the fall guy? Perhaps it might be useful to think of Richard as a figure in his own tragedy: does he have a fatal flaw that causes his demise, and can we work this into the plot in a concrete way?

General points:
At this stage it is my inclination to build up the characters – and their interrelationships – especially so if the characters are the embodiment of certain philosophical ideas – if they are, in essence, mythological. I would suggest working up the characters, and working up their story, and then paring the plot down to only what is essential within it. [...]

Can we work on the complexity within each scene? Can we make the relationships more ambiguous? They seem to be a little one-note at the moment. Except for the scene between Richard and Catherine in the hospital, the dynamic between characters rarely changes within a scene. (Incidentally, I notice that almost all of them are between two people only; there are very few group scenes). Like I say, I believe Richard is too passive and that Helen is two-dimensional – and this is where the plot suffers.

Can we envisage a dilemma for Henry that is fraught with anxiety because the consequences will be specific and immediately felt (and not just by Henry)? At the moment, if Henry does not receive this money then he does not go to university – the consequences are diffuse, varied and not immediately felt. It is difficult to feel the urgency for this money when it is simply for Henry's education (a character we do not know at all).

Would it be effective drama if we suspect all along that Helen might do something terrible to influence things in her favour? Could we be aware of the opportunities and possibilities for her; could there be a foreshadowing? This would become her internal struggle and it would become ours too: we yearn for things to fall in her favour and yet we also dread that she might do something immoral and unworthy in order to achieve those ends (a good person does a bad thing for a good reason), while also partly hoping that she will do it anyway. She would be presented with both external and internal frustrations to her plan of action.

Ultimately, however, could we come to realise that the conclusion was inevitable? The characters, their actions, the situation, it all made the conclusion the only one possible. The only question is how and when they arrive at this conclusion – in other words, the plot is made up of a constant blend of anticipation and uncertainty.

Following on from the idea in the paragraph above, should it be a possibility that Helen knows that Richard will decline her request (because of some act from the past – the sins of the father?) And that we know what the consequences will be, that some act from the past makes the conclusion to this current situation inevitable. [...]

Can we find an alternative way for Helen to discover the means of the murder? Discovering the Viagra article in the encyclopaedia seems to be a weak way for her to be presented with the opportunity. Is it not a compulsion for Helen to murder Richard? Perhaps someone else, Catherine or Henry maybe, should inadvertently present her with the opportunity?

Would it be worth splitting up the scene in which Richard tells Helen that he will not provide the money? Can Helen not find out about the news in some other way? Then we can take advantage of the tension as she prepares to confront him about it. At the moment, Helen finds out the information in the same scene in which she confronts Richard about it. Don't you feel we're missing an opportunity here?

Fold the exposition scenes (Helen visits Dan; Henry needs something etc.) into the drama – this will make it denser. [...]

Helen is dependent on Richard, and Dan is dependent on Helen. In what way are they similar in the positions of power – what does Helen want from her family?

* * *

I understand that many of my questions and suggestions tend towards archetypal tragedy and you might find that inauthentic or unjustified. However, you might find it instructive that that is how I understood the idea on its first reading; it seemed like a tragedy that needed development.

With kindest regards,
Oliver

2. Second Letter

Dear Oliver,

It was with close attention and great interest that I read your comments. Thank you for such thorough analysis and criticism and also for the ideas and proposals which you expressed regarding changes in the concept of the film. It is possible that we shall bear some of this in mind in our further work on the story of 'Helen'.

We should, however, like to say that in our view, the concept as a whole does not require any broadening of the limits already in existence, regardless of which aspect is under consideration: biography, characters of those in the main roles, their motivation, actions, relationships, the time and place of the action. We feel sure that all this is already present in this story to a sufficient and essential degree. Most importantly of all this applies to the Spirit of the film. The story was written in a single breath, swept along by inspiration. Any further deliberate structuring will, we feel, destroy that Spirit. Our writers' team has stood the test of time and is close-knit thanks to years of shared creative work, friendship and interdependence. We have been creating a world of our own in art, speaking a language of our own. We firmly stand by the principle: creation is the prerogative of authors. In other words that there should be no intervention by the producer (or whoever else it might be) in the creative process: that is the absolute and essential principle for our work. The most appropriate word for explaining this firm principle is the word 'trust'. You have to trust in our sensitivity and experience as authors, just as we are planning to put our trust in your sensitivity and talent as a producer. That is, of course, if you want to receive this film by Andrey Zvyagintsev and not something quite different. Why invite round a stone-mason and tell him how he ought to lay stones one on top of the other?

We feel sure that a script is only a technical record of what is going on in a film. It is an interim product on the path to a film and should not in any way be regarded as a finished work. Only when it has become a film – complete with light and shade, sets, compositions, colour, the essential natures of the actors, sunshine and darkness – does this material acquire true life.

In view of this we suggest that we need to clarify the crux of the matter: are we going to embark on a shared voyage with the story 'Helen' in its current form or not? We, of course, bear in mind that at the stage when the script is being created and the preparatory work on the film is in progress, certain changes are bound to surface in the overall concept of the film, dictated by our inspiration as authors and possibly called forth by your comments.

We look forward to your reply.
Yours sincerely,
Andrey Zvyagintsev, Oleg Negin, Mikhail Krichman

3. Third Letter

Dear Andrey, Oleg and Mikhail,
Many thanks for your letter and indeed for voicing your concerns with such honesty and conviction. I like very much what you say in your letter. Let me say immediately: you have complete creative freedom.

I approached you for this project because I admire your films and I would like your film with us to be a Zvyagintsev film. It is neither my place nor my intention to interfere in your right to create the film that you deem necessary. You might remember what we said in our initial proposal to you: you have complete creative freedom with this project. You also have final cut. Please do not feel you have to argue for it; it is our arrangement that you have it already. It is not an issue.

However, it is clear that you are taken aback by my comments. Really, the main point to make is that, just because I give you my comments, it does not mean that I am telling you what to do or how to do it. It does not mean that I do not trust you. As you say, it serves neither of us to do each other's job. Nevertheless, it is the duty of the producer to get the best from the director and his team. It serves the film for me to provoke and encourage you, to push you. I hope you noted that I did not push you in one particular direction or another, and I certainly did not make any remarks about any meaning within the film. In short, make of my comments what you will; they were simply a reaction. Ultimately, it is for you to make the decisions about your film and it is for me to support your decisions.

Before I address 'Helen' in particular I would like to make one rather banal point: we do have a responsibility to balance commercial needs with artistic needs. You may choose to see me as the personification of the undesirable needs of the market. In reality, there is not much I can do about them. They exist and they cannot be ignored. But, to use your point about being road-tested, my expertise is the international film market – I know who buys what and for what price; and I know that I have devised a framework that allows you to have creative freedom and for me to satisfy the needs of the market.

So, while you have complete creative freedom, we do need to agree at the outset on a project that fits the framework. Which brings me to 'Helen' in particular:

As you know, I like 'Helen'. I think it has much promise. With its ideas and story, it makes very interesting use of the apocalypse theme. If this is the film that you want to make then I am happy to accept it. I say that sincerely. However, it does not quite fit the scope of our initial proposal to you – certainly, 'Helen' would not have a budget that even approaches $6-7m. Subsequently, we would have to arrange for a completely different financial package. So, in this light, I think these are the options:

- we go ahead with 'Helen' as part of the apocalypse project but at the appropriate budget. Or...
- we put 'Helen' to one side and you, Oleg and Mikhail think of another idea that makes full use of the scope of our proposal. Naturally, we want you to be excited by this scope. Just to give you an example: 'Grapes' has a broader scope than 'Helen' and, from what I understand, it was still an idea completely of your own devising. It did not quite fit our proposal because of the particulars of its story but I hope you see what I mean. Or...
- We make a deal where we make two films, one to fit more clearly the scope of the apocalypse proposal and then, as a completely separate film and according to your wishes, 'Helen'. Of course, both films will be entirely Zvyagintsev films.

I am sure you will want to take some time to reflect on this. Personally, I am happy with all of those options.

Whatever you decide you would like to do, I hope you understand that you have my support. I believe we share the same conception of what film is and how films should be made. They are made in a spirit of trust and respect. You can have no doubt that you have my complete trust and respect.

With kindest regards,
Oliver

4. Fourth Letter

Hi Oliver!
Firstly I should like to congratulate you on what is possibly one of the most important events in life. Greetings and congratulations to your chosen bride!

I am very pleased and had not previously doubted that we should reach a common understanding. I agree with you completely that in order to make a film it is imperative to achieve an atmosphere of trust and mutual respect. For my part, I assure you, Oliver, that if I had not felt respect and trust for you I should not have made so bold as to use such an open and sincere tone in my previous letter.

So – to the heart of the matter... After thinking it over, we are inclined to opt for the first of the options you suggested to us. In other words we see 'Helen' as the only plan, which not only inspires us (and we are eagerly looking forward to implementing it) but also fits in with the idea of the 'Apocalypse' and complies with the essential conditions laid down for the project: the English language and West-European/American actors. Other ideas – on a wider scale perhaps – we see as exclusively Russian (from the language point of view) and so for the moment we see little point in discussing them at this stage.

In view of this, Oliver, we should like to start concrete negotiations about when this collaboration should start. First of all we should like to receive from you information regarding amendment of the budget – your thoughts on the matter and some rough figures. We would also be grateful if you would put forward a plan for our joint action.

In short I propose that we should venture forth on this voyage and at last set sail. So that none of us should lose any precious time,

I have done a simple calculation of how many days have been spent on exchanging letters and it turns out (naturally on account of unavoidable circumstances) that in the period from March 12th up to now (March 29th) we have written each other only three letters and I feel it is essential to start communicating more intensively and perhaps in a different form – on Skype for instance with an interpreter...

With best wishes.
Yours sincerely, Andrey & Co.

After that letter there was a pause resulting from the need to draw up a contract. Soon after that we received a contract from Oliver in English. For understandable reasons the text of that contract has not been included in this publication. After receiving it, I sent Oliver a detailed letter which follows below:

5. Fifth Letter

Dear Oliver,
I have acquainted myself with the text of the contract and have to admit that I feel at a loss. I want you to know where I stand before you receive the text of the contract drawn up in response to yours by Daniel[3]. I should like to express in writing how I was taken aback, breaking the text down into its component parts. Here goes:

1. The first surprise is bound up with the following statement in the text of the contract which you (the Company) proposed (I quote): "In connection with the payment made to the Director of the sum of $5,000 of which he acknowledges receipt, the parties have agreed to the following: 1. The Company hereby recognises that the Director *has already created and transmitted* to the Company a Synopsis entitled 'Helen'."

In my opinion this text contradicts that dated 2:02:2009, 'A Proposal for AZ' (I quote): "The Director *receives a one-off payment*

---

[3] Daniel Goroshko – a Russian film distributor. In the first stages of the *Elena* project he acted as our legal consultant.

of $5,000 for agreeing to take part in the work on the Project". The contradiction is obvious. I agreed to take part in the project a long time ago and I still plan to wait till July (as the two of us had already agreed verbally) and therefore I regard the proposed sum as recognition for the time I have spent waiting for this project to take shape and the opportunities for embarking on another project which has accordingly been dropped. Then again, how can the above-mentioned sum be regarded as an option or advance for the proposed script of 'Helen', which was written by another person, namely my co-author, Oleg Negin? I do not understand.

2. I have stressed on more than one occasion in our conversations and letters that I regard the text of 'Helen' as a script. Of course it requires more work, more details and additions, after which it will be possible to refer to the future text as *the Director's Script*, but you (the Company) refer to the text of 'Helen' as *a synopsis*.

If you are worried about the size of the text, I make so bold as to assure you that the number of pages in a script says very little about the duration of the eventual film. Even if we were to turn the text of 'Helen' now into a so-called 'American version' with the appropriate font size and intervals between the lines, we would end up with possibly 60 pages. The script of the film *The Banishment* consisted of 35 pages (it was printed in exactly the same way as the text of 'Helen' sent to you consisting of 25 pages) and by the way *The Banishment*, as you know, lasts two and a half hours. In a word I regard the text for 'Helen' sent to you as *a literary script* for a full-length film of approximately 90 minutes' duration.

3. You write in the contract (I quote): "the Director retains the right to the *final cut*, bearing in mind the rights enjoyed by the financial backers".

Short comment: in my opinion it has to be one or the other – either the Director's right or that of the financial backers. This needs clarifying.

4. In the contract (I quote): "At the request of the Company, the Director together with the co-author will make such changes and corrections in the Script and/or shall write further versions of the Script which the Company *requests*".

Now to turn to some fragments from your letter, Oliver (I quote): "I want to dispel your doubts: you retain complete creative freedom.

[...] I should like the film that you present me with precisely to be a film by Zvyagintsev. I do not plan in any way to restrict your right to create a film in accordance with your own ideas. You will remember that in our initial proposal we guaranteed you complete creative freedom within the framework of this project... I hope you have noted that I am not trying in any way at all to steer your creative work in any specific direction... After all, it is you who takes the final decisions regarding this film and my task to support the decisions you take... There should not be any differences between us on this subject". In my opinion the differences are obvious.

The next point also links in with the ideas expressed in connection with Point 4.

5. In the contract it is written (I quote): "After receiving the script, the Company will have it translated into English and, on condition that there are consultations with the Director on the subject, shall be entitled to appoint an Anglophone writer to make the necessary changes and additions to the translation of the text in the script".

As we see it, this *writer* needs, naturally, not just to be a translator – as was appropriately indicated in the text of the contract – but definitely a person capable of adapting dialogues and certain nuances in the action within the narrative, starting out from the culture of the country, in which it is planned that the shooting of the film 'Helen' should take place. At the same time, bearing in mind the content of the previous point in this letter, I deem it necessary to point out *the subsidiary nature* of such *a writer*. He provides consultations and interacts closely with the authors of the script, not in keeping with indications or recommendations from any other parties. I am interested in such an arrangement only if it functions like that between me and my co-author, Oleg Negin.

6. In the contract there is not a single word about the time-span involved in this agreement. It would seem to me that it would be correct to specify time limits (anticipation of the transformation of a dream into reality cannot last indefinitely). If we do not get the project off the ground in July 2009 (when I say 'off the ground' I do not mean the time when the parties start to finalise their agreements, but when we start shooting the film: searching for locations, casting, work by designers, scriptwriters, the camera-man and the whole crew – in a word organisational work), then it will not be possible to

shoot anything in February/March, to edit in April/May, to sort out the sound in June and then the project is no longer attractive for me, because I have other commitments in 2011.

7. The last and perhaps the most important point. On April 6th when we were negotiating via Skype, we agreed that in July 2009 we could start on the preparatory stage of the 'Helen' project and from that I drew the conclusion that the *Company had decided* to develop further and launch the 'Helen' project. If that is the case, then why in Point 11 of the contract is there the following statement: "If *for any reason*, the Company – during consultations with the Director decides *at any stage* that the 'Helen' Synopsis is inappropriate for further development or production, the Director will have the right to compile up to three alternative synopses appropriate for the Series..." I have to say that I am not prepared for any such adventures – to start work and then 'for any reason' and 'at any stage' to interrupt the project. Work of that kind was never part of my plans. I take on a project only when I'm sure that I've made the right choice and I expect an equally responsible attitude from others. Are you (the Company) ready to take on this project or not? As I see it the question has to be decided now, definitely not any later.

I received a proposal for collaboration from the Company at the very beginning of February and recently agreed to wait for the finance until the beginning of July. In July it will be exactly six months since I received your first letter 'A Proposal for AZ' with the suggestion (I remember a part of it): "We plan to start work on the production of the film in 2010. In other words, each director will have at least a year to prepare for shooting the film and assembling a film crew." As you can see, there is only half of that year left. Furthermore: not only do I find myself depending on three other directors and the inner rhythm of their lives, which – as I see it – raises doubts with regard to any guarantee that we shall be able to start work in July, but the Company also retains the right to reject the project 'for any reason' or 'at any stage'. Months of happy hopes and expectations have passed by and then suddenly I read in the contract that the Company can still have second thoughts. You must agree that such an uncertain situation makes it imperative to look for more reliable sources of support. I consider the text of the script for 'Helen' as material which does not belong to anyone other than its authors. I am waiting for a clearer and more transparent expression of the Company's intentions and time schedule. Oliver, please understand me properly and answer the questions I have raised as soon as possible (if you can, in the course of next week). On May 13th the Cannes Festival opens. If we fail to achieve a proper level of mutual understanding, I do not want to pass up chances to look for other sources of finance for the 'Helen' project in the context of encounters at Cannes.

Yours sincerely,
Andrey

P.S. I am available for discussions on Skype or e-mail at any time.

6. Sixth Letter

Dear Andrey,
Many thanks for your letter. I have tried to answer all your questions and respond to all your points in the letter below. My numbers correspond to the numbers of your points. Let me start though with what may be the essential point. If you have an opportunity to get 'Helen' into production with a producer or entity other than our company, and on a schedule faster than us, then it would be grossly unfair of us to prevent you from taking that opportunity. It is very difficult to raise finance for independent films at the moment and we feel a filmmaker must be free to make the most of his opportunities.

In this light, you might welcome the following proposition: you and Oleg discuss the project with other potential producers – if they can put the film into production according to your time frame then you must do so; if your search proves unsuccessful then of course there is always the chance that we can still collaborate in 2010. In short, I appreciate that we are not moving as fast as you would like but, as I will explain, nothing has changed in the original schedule.

You rightly point out that the film depends on the involvement of three other filmmakers. We find ourselves in a difficult position: our filmmakers are working at very different paces. Naturally, we expected different rhythms but not to such a degree. In all honesty, you presented your idea far quicker than we imagined and, thanks to your natural methods, you are not looking to develop the scenario as might be expected of a traditional or 'American' script. There is a large difference between a writer developing his script and a whole team of department heads working in preparation for 6-7 months (i.e July to February). The expense will be significant, akin to pre-production rather than development. This has never been part of our schedule.

There are still two months between now and July. Much may happen in those two months of course but I cannot reasonably guarantee that we will have everything in place for you to start your operations by then and certainly not on the scale that you suggest - hence my proposition in the second paragraph. It is still our intention to put the four films into production at some stage in 2010; nothing has changed in that respect. When we spoke on the telephone I said that I was aiming to have the package in place by July – by that I meant having the four filmmakers signed on and having some finance in place for the development of the projects (as you know, I was happy for you to scout some locations to develop 'Helen' in the meantime).

Nothing has changed in this respect either. Let me state very clearly though: this is an aim, it is not a guarantee. I see little point in offering you a deadline, and certainly not when we are sticking to our original schedule. Instead, however, we are prepared to offer you the flexibility to approach other sources of support for 'Helen' in the interim.

Now, it might be the case that you and Oleg approach other producers for 'Helen' but then in, say, October 2009 we return to you with the necessary finance for you to start the whole process (which would give you about 5 months of preparation if you want to film in February). You would then have the opportunity to accept or decline our invitation. How do you feel about that prospect? We feel it is a fair proposal that reflects honestly the positions we are both in.

I am afraid I cannot be forced to give you specific deadlines – frankly, they are beyond my control – but I can offer you this flexibility. As we say in English, you cannot have your cake and eat it.

Now, to address your points:

1. The $5000 is dependent on the signing of this agreement. The intention of the agreement is to establish the broad outline of our collaboration and to protect both of us within the agreement. The

$5000 is not linked specifically to the delivery of 'Helen'; it is linked to the fact that we have come to an agreement to work together. You will see that this stipulation was included in the first version of the agreement (dated the 27th February), when there was no mention of 'Helen' at all – Daniel acknowledged receipt of this first agreement but never followed up with his comments. We incorporate 'Helen' into the latest agreement simply to reflect the progress and conversations since that version of 27th February.

2. I understand. It seems the misunderstanding lies in the fact that I thought we had agreed on the story of 'Helen' but that you were going to develop, refine and improve it. And I assumed that that process would require successive drafts. By that, I do not mean that we were necessarily expecting a 120 page script; we quite understand you have your own methods but we expected that you would work towards something that might be termed a 'script', as opposed to the 'scenario' that exists at the moment. I hope that explains the language in the agreement.

3. You have final cut, there is no issue here. This line in the agreement reflects the possibility that we will secure a completion guarantor for the film as insurance for the backers. In the event that a completion guarantor steps in to take control of the film then they assume the right to either finish the film as best they can or repay the investors – in that instance then, contractually, they would have final cut.

4. In the context of a typical screenplay, it is quite normal for there to be successive drafts and, contractually, somebody must have the right to determine whether the script is ready for production or not. In practice, of course, the decision is made together and both director and producer must be happy with the decision – which is a question of trust and understanding. (It is perhaps a deficiency of any contractual agreement that it is very difficult to reflect the idea of trust.) This clause does not mean that the producer can ask the writers to insert a specific piece of dialogue, for example. So, I do not agree that there is a conflict between the filmmaker having creative control over his film and the producer retaining the right to determine its readiness for production. The producer does not tell the filmmaker how to make his film – I think I have made that point clearly enough. Similarly, however, the filmmaker remains

accountable to the producer – for, in turn, the producer is accountable to the investors, the market and, ultimately, the audience. The simple truth is that no investor would back a film in which the producer did not have control over such a fundamental issue. It is understandable that directors are nervous of this idea – but it is to the detriment of the film and the whole production process if there is not a clear understanding of this dynamic. The process is a collaboration in which each person is given the confidence to do their job by the other. This must surely be the ideal scenario for making a film. As I have said many times, you have my confidence.

5. Of course, as the director, it is for you to determine the nature of your relationship with your creative partners – the same goes for co-writers as it does for any other contributor. I have not suggested the name of any writer to you. On the contrary, I have asked if there are any writers in the English language with whom you would like to collaborate. We are more than happy to make suggestions.

7. This clause is actually to protect you, not us. It is only there in the event that you decide you want to make another story – you might feel that 'Helen' is not developing as well as you expected and you wish to change direction, or you might discover another idea that you prefer. This clause gives you the option to stay with our project. It is about giving you flexibility. What I say in point 4 applies here equally.

I hope that answers your queries and doubts. I am sure you will want to reflect on this matter for a few days. For my part, I am continuing to put the whole package together and, naturally, we are delighted you are part of it.

With kindest regards,
Oliver

This was followed by telephone conversations, which, overall, turned out to be of little or no avail. It was clear that Oliver's quite interesting 'Apocalypse' project was strategically flawed. How can you synchronise the life goals, rhythms and everyday schedules of 4 directors as if they were one? Plus assembling such a portfolio for investors is daunting, not to mention the fact that when you consider Oliver's meticulousness and his incessant questions about every last detail of our script, even at the first stage, I can hardly imagine what he would have done with four full-length scripts in his hands. Would he really have sent all of them the same type of detailed commentaries as those with which he'd honoured our humble project? In short, I realised that we were wasting our time. That this neverending tête-à-tête was impossible, and therefore elected to sever relations. We parted on quite friendly terms – I had a telephone conversation with him, I apologised and said that it would be too much of a luxury for me to sit with ready script and wait for God knows how much time for God knows what. Oliver reacted to the situation with understanding, I took the script back and sent him the final letter in this correspondence.

7. Seventh Letter

Dear Oliver,
Thank you for the understanding you have shown by suggesting that I feel free to seek alternative sources of finance for the 'Helen' project. I am now handing another producer the Russian and English versions. I hope that you won't be against this.
If my searches prove unsuccessful, the possibility of you and I working together in 2010 remains. I'm always ready to consider new work, as you know. I shall send you a more detailed letter later on, because I still have some questions I want to ask you.

Once again, thank you for your understanding.
Yours sincerely,
Andrey

Such was the story of the birth and travails of the 'Elena' idea. Very soon, after some unsuccessful attempts to reach agreements over finance in Russia, I met Alexander Rodnyansky and, at the end of August 2009, he and I 'shook hands on a deal'. No more than a month later, at the beginning of October, we embarked on the pre-production for the film. The plan had come back home, to the familiar realities of Russian life, and I was glad at the outcome. I am happy to have met Alexander, a remarkably educated and very interesting man, a true intellectual. Relations between us were soon rooted in mutual understanding and after the first few meetings, they had – I would say – developed into the kind of relations I am familiar with and am used to, relations on whose banner I would write the word 'Trust'. I did not need to insist on my right to perceive the world in my own way, to portray it in my own language. I no longer needed to prove to anyone that the narrative required a specific shape and not just any shape or rhythm. I could breathe freely. That is real happiness – to be able to be free in your creative endeavours.

I came across this correspondence with the British producer by chance, but then I remembered that, not long after he and I had broken off relations, I had been telling someone how I had met a remarkable man from London but that unfortunately the film had come to nothing purely because of the time-scale required. I added other things as well and was not conscious of lying. I told the story just as it was, as I remembered it, recalling the after-taste of that period which had lasted three or four months. Now, however, as I have been re-reading these letters I am horrified to realise what was lying in wait for me in that oh-so-sweet mouse-trap. (I had been offered a project with a budget of seven million dollars and tempting promises as regards fees and hefty royalties).

The young producer is a remarkable man, but how right I had been to decide not to work with him! I would have been burnt out like a candle, answering his everlasting questions which were important only to him. It's possible that the laborious task of answering his questions would have left me no time for asking myself the simplest and most obvious question of all: what was the point of my answering them? The venture would have ended in disaster. I can see this all too clearly now.

THE DIRECTOR'S PRODUCTION DIARY.
ANDREY ZVYAGINTSEV

THE DIRECTOR'S PRODUCTION DIARY[4]

Thursday, October 8, 2009
The beginning. Work has commenced on this account and the film *Elena*.

For more than a month Oleg[5] and I have been 'squatting' in this office, polishing the script. Our Moleskin pads have been purchased and we're on our way. It's been a difficult day and it was an uphill job to crawl as far as Episode 70 – the conversation between the doctor from the ambulance service and Elena. It was a struggle to get the atmosphere right. We came to a conclusion, which had basically always been clear. Yet it was only today that it took shape of its own accord so to speak. In this part of the script (and in the film as well) we are dealing with figures embodying a message and not with socially 'authentic', real human beings.

Actors, whether we like it or not, will always make these characters come to life. Anything else would be impossible. Yet it is unnecessary to justify absolutely all the nuances and twists through an analysis of how 'true-to-life' the characters are and look for a psychologically precise match between their behaviour and any prototype drawn from real life in a similar situation. This script is not a document. It is not a short-hand record of the feelings of a real live individual with an 'authentic' life-story. Who is Vladimir? How did he earn all that money? What does Sergei do with himself? Perhaps we should hang a security guard's jacket in his hall? What kind of a woman is his wife Tatiana? How does Katerina earn her living? Where does

---

[4] This text is published in the director's version.

[5] Oleg Negin – Scriptwriter.

she live? With whom? etc. Questions of that kind are not necessary here and we do not need to weave a fabric for a real narrative. It's not built for coping with questions like that: they would just bring down the whole structure of the edifice. (Incidentally some passages in Chekhov's plays could not stand up to analysis of that kind either.) What difference does it make whether Sergei works as a security guard or is just a moonlighter? Perhaps he doesn't work anywhere at all. Limiting the options narrows down rather than broadens the *character*. One look at his face ought to be enough to convey what kind of person he is. People are signs, which are recognisable and comprehensible just as easily after their first few remarks as after a first hard look at them. The key things are spot-on casting, together with a precise story-line and dialogue. As far as the dramatic presentation is concerned it is as laconic and plain as possible, the subject moves strictly towards its dénouement without deviation. The plot is conveyed in broad sweeps and is not bogged down in detail or any chewing over of the circumstances, justifications or any other kind of unnecessary explanations of various murky sequences.

The day before I started this diary Oleg and I spent all the daylight hours in the basement of the office working on the script. By today (having started out on September 1st or 2nd) we have got as far as Episode 55. The scene where Vladimir and Elena have already spoken about the inheritance, about the Kingdom of Heaven and "the last shall be first." As a matter of fact, we're approaching the end. All the main dialogues are behind us. All that remains is action and a small number of purely functional (as regards dialogue) scenes. There is still no ending. We're waiting for it to be born... In the evening there was the première of *NYILY*[6]. A shameful business. It would be difficult to imagine anything worse...

Two days before I started this diary was a landmark day, when Melkumov[7] paid a visit to our ramshackle office. He looked round cautiously, unable to understand why we had preferred to work in

---

[6] *NYILY - New York I Love You* (2009) – a film from which the novella contributed by Andrey Zvyagintsev with the title *Apocrypha* was omitted. When the film was shown in Russia, the distribution company decided to screen *Apocrypha* separately, before the main version of the film.

[7] Sergey Melkumov – producer from the company 'Non-Stop Production', which financed the film *Elena*.

this basement instead of the Mosfilm studios, until he went up a floor and saw the other three or four rooms. We discussed the contract for the script. We fought (quietly) over the points on which our views differed. On one side there were Oleg and I and on the producer's side Melkumov and his lawyer. We also discussed opportunities for working in Germany. Baumgartner[8] and five days' shooting in Germany...

Friday, October 9, 2009
The day got off to a really bad start. Oleg and I were driving for the nth time during the last month from his house to the office along Sivtsev Vrazhek Lane to 10 Plotnikov Lane, when a call came through from Melkumov. He informed us that it would be unlikely we would be able officially to start work before the end of October. That meant that we, of course, would continue to work, but it would be difficult to have everything ready from the official point of view before the end of October. "Ekaterina[9] should meet up with Olga[10] on Monday and give her the job of making the payments for what has to be dealt with immediately: furniture, Internet, crew members etc., etc." Once again more delays... all this has a horrible impact on the whole atmosphere. It makes it impossible to maintain a healthy creative environment. I've taken a break. If the most pressing issues have not been settled by Monday, I shall probably have to just sidestep Melkumov and demand that we review the conditions for the project with Rodnyansky. To hell with them all!

    BWV 847 – Prelude No. 2 in C Minor from Book 1 of *The Well-Tempered Clavier* (in C minor) performed by Glen Gould. After the opening credits this music is heard in complete darkness like an introduction or entrance into the story. A preamble to set the mood, a 'cushion'. "Now you shall see a story full of tragedy..."

Saturday, October 10, 2009
The whole of the first half of the day we spent on the contract for

---

[8] Karl Baumgartner – film distributor and producer, with whom negotiations were going on about a co-production during the first weeks of work on *Elena*.

[9] Ekaterina Marakulina – Executive Producer.

[10] Olga Kudryavtseva – production director of the company 'Non-Stop Production'.

the script. We wrote a scathing letter to Kudryavtseva, which she'd deserved. How much time has to be spent on all this nonsense? But on the other hand it trains the mind and keeps us up to the mark.

The golden section. Episodes 60-72... the scenes where the crime is conceived and carried out. We numbered the episodes in the script which came to a total of 96. I was sure that today we would finish the work on polishing the script. We got stuck on Episode 95. The scene by the electricity meter. "The end of the world is over!" We tied up the dialogue between Sergei and his neighbour. It didn't seem to hang together properly. On the other hand we came up with some interesting details for the episode in the suburban electric train (with the horse): the voice over the loud-speaker and the empty carriage. Then there were some fine touches in the scene back at Sergei's flat... "Mama, mama... Let's drink to that." The baby crying... It was late when we stopped work.

Anya came to fetch us. She waited for us in silence, till we had finished working.

Sunday, October 11, 2009
Oleg rang really early at 9:30 and made me get up. Admittedly I went back to sleep till 10:00... But by 12 we were in Plotnikov Lane.

Mikhail, who happened to be in Arbat Street, looked in briefly. He came in with a pram with a sleeping infant in it. I say infant, because the four-week-old lad hasn't been given a name yet...

A red-letter day. Today at a quarter past two we finished the script. 96 episodes. 62 pages. In a few days we'll get working on the filming-time schedule and tomorrow we'll start working with Mikhail[11] on the direction. We've got a whole day in front of us. We can go out for a bit and then come back to work on the contracts for the script and the direction. Then at some stage after six I'll go and see Ivan with Fyodor...

A sad day – we've finished the script and there won't be any more sitting here and working together. Now there are going to be different days and different people. Oleg is in a state of contented melancholy...

---

[11] Mikhail Krichman – Director of Photography.

Monday, October 12, 2009
The first day of work with Mikhail. A large part of the day we spent talking about a name for his son. In general about the difficult question of choosing a name for a child. We warmed up and then turned to the script. The day went well. It was like the old days when things had gone well, forgotten moments of shared creativity. The blessed time when we can get down to work is just round the corner... It's a fine feeling. In the evening Ekaterina Marakulina rang to share the good news about the financial talks going well. The discussion part is already over. We'll have the furniture by the end of the week, Internet and other facilities. Once we're that far, we can start hiring people for the project. We're off...

On Thursday or Friday there'll be a meeting of the initial team with Melkumov (at his suggestion). This is good news – an initiative of that kind from the producer is a good sign. We'll see how this bodes for the future. In the next few days I'm to meet Elina[12]. She is due to make proposals for the second 'tranche' of the actors. After a list has been drawn up, we'll start meeting them and recording short interviews with them on camera. We need to see how they look now. Photographs from the Internet are not always up-to-date. Things seem to have taken off at last. God be with us.

Tuesday, October 13, 2009
The day began in Starbucks on Arbat Street. Hot chocolate and Krichman turning up late. A good day nonetheless. So far we're naturally only finding our way into the film, but there's already a good feel about it. We seem to be moving. Some good ideas were put forward today. Apart from everyhing else the infant's a month old today. Soon he'll have to acquire a name according to the relatives who are pushing and persuading.

Then we had that ridiculous outfit 'TOP-Film' turning up with talk of the premiere and working with the press. The sooner we get that behind us the better. Tomorrow they're planning to squeeze 18 interviews into a mere two hours. Idiots. Tomorrow will be terrible!!! I was tired and arrived home in the evening ready to drop. I'm taking the day off tomorrow. Then in the evening we'll face the idiots.

---

[12] Elina Ternyaeva – Casting Director.

Friday, October 16, 2009
Mikhail wasn't there today. So I worked with Oleg instead and we finished off the script contract. Recently I've had the feeling that we get together to write contracts rather than scripts. The script though is more or less finished. Yet I feel there isn't an ending yet. The ending with the little girl and *The Well-tempered Clavier* I really liked, but I have to say that not everyone did. Many people found it unsatisfactory. I'm not as enthusiastic about it now either.

I lost my cool in the end and telephoned Ekaterina, Rodnyansky's secretary. Without laying on any pressure or pathos of the righteous, I said very calmly that "I was requesting a meeting for the three of us: Rodnyansky, Melkumov and myself. As soon as possible..." That was all.

No more than an hour later, Melkumov – out of character – telephoned Marakulina and started asking how things were going, why we weren't taking on any staff, what stage the work was at and so on. Usually he rings me directly, ignoring Ekaterina, but on this occasion he talked to her straightaway. One might compare his response to 'a cat on a hot tin roof' but I feel the term might be too optimistic in his case... Nevertheless, people were beginning to move, to start working... There's going to be a meeting next week.

We went home at 22:30. Oleg was sitting in the front, next to the driver as always. I was in the back. A call came through from Anya. "It's starting, my love..." At 23:15 I was already in hospital reception.

I walk home in the rain. Everything's fine. We exchange text messages throughout the night. "As soon as you have the strength to lie back on the delivery table and write, let me know whatever is happening, won't you?" I think to myself that if it wasn't for the iPhone it would be harder to tap in the letters.

All night until 7:00 a.m. I was on Skype with Oleg and exchanging text messages with Anya...

At 7:40 Pyotr was born. Pyotr Andreyevich was born at 7:40 on October 17th. He weighed in at 3.440 kilos and measured 52cms.

Tuesday, October 20, 2009
Fortunately it turned out that, thanks to the press showing of *New York I Love You* there was a chance to keep an eye on the release of a print of our 'novella'. And also to make sure that the sound was

mixed in Dolby Surround Sound. Some technical mishap had taken place but nobody seemed to know anything about what had caused it. The sound synchronisation was all over the place which meant the novella was unrecognisable. The sound quality was horrifically bad. The dubbing was simply ghastly, devoid of any taste or talent. Today I managed to get on top of all that. Hurray! Pafnutii[13] and a sound-producer responsible for synchronisation called Sergei (I don't know which) straightened it all out in the Peking Hotel in the Shufutinsky studios. We threw out two meaningless remarks from the dubbed text, one of which had appeared from heaven knows where. How people can work like that just amazes me: the author of the script and the film's director live here in Russia within 'easy reach' in Moscow. Surely they could have phoned and asked how the text should sound in a particular part of the film. Damn those part-timers and bunglers!

That same evening Andrey Ponkratov[14] and I came to the maternity hospital and brought Anya and Pyotr home. Some old man down in reception pushed a photograph under my nose full of pink babies and the silly faces of their mothers and offered us a photo session. When I refused his offer straight out, he looked at me in complete astonishment and said: "Well, that's silly..."

Back home. My mother, Natasha's, Anya and Pyotr, Ponkratov and me... The Supreme Assembly celebrated with Armagnac 1974.

Wednesday, October 21, 2009
In the afternoon I went to the Gorky Studios, hoping to be able to solve the problem with the print: in what I had seen to date the contrasts were too stark: the whole scene in the bus (with the boy against the background of the window) seemed to consist of silhouettes with virtually no detail. It's a long section and if there are no details of his face when certain important things are reflected in the nuances of his acting, that makes it difficult to watch. The screen seems empty for a long time. It was important to establish whether it was a projection problem or just a bad print. As usual in this world, you're sent off "heaven knows where" to do "heaven knows what"... On this occasion as well, we (Mikhail and I) were told at Gorky Studios that they had

---

[13] Andrey Dergachev (Pafnutii) – Sound Producer.

[14] Andrey Ponkratov – Art Director.

not been expecting us and that they were not planning a print run before the next day or the day after that... The only thing that we did achieve was to see the reference (standard) copy of the New York 'novella'.

I met up with Elina at 16:00. She showed me photographs from the Internet for the actors she was proposing. Photos of Elena, Vladimir and Katerina... Today we reached a decision to move on two fronts, creating a base for two projects so to speak: (a) a gathering of stars – Menshov, Govorukhin, Porokhovshchikov, Khamatova, Rappoport etc. and (b) a group of little known actors – one from Saratov (recommended by Igor Savochkin) and a young, little-known actress for Katerina and Nadezhda Markina, for example, for Elena...

At 18:00 four of us went to meet Rodnyansky in his office: Melkumov, Rodnyansky, Ekaterina Marakulina and me... There were no arguments, not even any particular complaints: indeed it seemed as if everybody had understood everything. Melkumov roused himself at last. It looks as if everything is going to be different now. If it isn't then it won't be peace any more, but war.

"The most *meaningful* element in language is not words themselves, but the tone, energy, modulation and tempo with which a series of words is uttered – in short the music underlying words, the passion underlying that music, the individual behind that passion: thus everything which cannot be written down..." – Nietzsche.

Thursday, October 22, 2009
A whole series of exhausting empty days (I'm looking back at them as I write this). Exhausting because of all the delays, the administrative bullshit, empty promises, deferred meetings – in other words, the 'putting-off-the-launch' strategy, which has perhaps been tried out and tested on others (rather like: "How long can I go on not feeding these people? They're not asking for food yet, perhaps we can force them to go hungry a little longer?"). It's such an Asiatic (or in fact Russian) way of working. It's difficult to even call it work. It's all f— ked up. If they would only say: "There's no money, there'll be some in after the 15th of November...". Then people would know that they still have months to wait. But no, they promised the moon at the beginning of September, using words like "absolutely definite" or telling them that "without a doubt we will be starting on October 5th

or 6th at the latest" and then led us a merry dance! The atmosphere utterly discourages creativity. Morale is low, everything's up in the air, nothing's definite and it all looks bad. All this time Mikhail and I tried to start working on the shot breakdown and we spent a few days moving up from the ground floor (basement) to the first, attempting to avoid the workmen assembling IKEA furniture and get out of their way, so as to at least get something started... Those were not the comfortable conditions Rodnyansky had promised us.

But now it looks as if everything's plain sailing at last... Thank God...

We're taking on staff with each passing day. The team is growing. Drivers have appeared. An office manager called Tatiana. My assistant Anastasia. The first days of casting are behind us... We have a location manager, Alexander Voronov, who is thorough, punctual and meticulous. The wheels are turning at last.

Wednesday, October 28, 2009
Today at last the work on the shot breakdown got off the ground. We decided how to shoot the first four episodes. The actual opening of the film seems clear now. So far I like very much the idea of a general view from the outside between the trunks of the trees coming down on to the balcony with large windows. It's a long shot. The sky lightens and the birds start waking up. It's cool. Possibly two crows will fly past the camera. An idea I had had while working on *The Banishment*[15], but have not used.

Yesterday we met up with Ponkratov who brought the plans for the layout of Vladimir's flat, and even some preliminary sketches of the space. Surprisingly, the very first proposal appeared really interesting. I was very taken with the idea. So far so good...

Thursday, October 29, 2009
Today, early in the morning, little Pyotr gave me such a beautiful smile that it even seemed as if it was something entirely conscious on his part. And this was on Day 12!

We have got as far as Episode 8. We've put off deciding how Episode 6 will look. Because of the camera movement involved,

---

[15] The film which Andrey Zvyagintsev made prior to *Elena* and released in 2007.

Mikhail is worried about my idea for a long take 'Vladimir waking up – opening the blinds in the bedroom, putting on his dressing gown, going down the corridor, bathroom, washing, Elena making Vladimir's bed and the exchange of greetings' all filmed like a vista using a curved dolly track. "We're moving around too much" was his comment. I like this idea very much indeed. Precisely because it's long and calm. We've decided to put off making a decision for the moment. We'll decide on it later or on set.

At 18:30 an actress called Masha (I don't remember which) auditioned. She is young, looks very like Drubich[16] and is 23. Perhaps this is an *extremely* young candidate for the part of Katerina. For some reason this idea of a young Katerina is proving a problem. At that age she would have no 'knowledge of life', no 'inner calm' or 'balance'. Where might she have acquired them from? A pleasant girl, animated, competent, very fresh... I need to think, to do another audition...

Anastasia Karasyova[17] has joined us. She's a pleasant girl and I hope she won't let us down... So far she has shown herself in a very positive light. She clearly seemed perturbed when she realised the kind of 'situation' she would have to deal with – all the colleagues, the Olegs, the Elinas, the Ekaterinas and an office overflowing with boxes.

At 20:20 I left for Domodedovo airport. Tomorrow I have to be in Novosibirsk, at the Pobeda Cinema... its -6°... On the way I chatted to Oleg mainly about his personal life and a little about the role of Katerina and the girl who he had seen earlier in the day, who was auditioning for the part... I'm sitting in the Costa café as I write these lines. It's take-off in 20 minutes. I ring dear Pyotr & Anya back home.

Friday, October 30, 2009
Novosibirsk airport stretches out below us. The steward informs us that we shall be landing in fifteen minutes. An idea for the ending!! The boy, Sasha, is walking with his mates (seen from the back) into some kind of impenetrable darkness... Uncertainty, confusion, chaos, nothing... Ex nihilo...

The next shot will have the same rhythm as the first shot of the

---

[16] Tatyana Drubich – a Russian actress.

[17] Anastasia Karasyova – Director's Assistant.

film... Elena is standing in front of a window in Sergei's flat. The camera is outside. We can see some windows (only a small number, so that we can still make out the features of her face...) In the foreground (we're on the first or second floor) there is the top of a street-lamp... As we are watching it, the street-lamp slowly lights up, 'starts burning', brighter and brighter... Ending/Fin.

A new sun. *God's Eclipse*... A yawning abyss – Void in front of which we find a human being of today, our contemporary. Truth, Goodness, Beauty have faded: "the divine light has gone out – terror has become our chief mirror. All that Man can find in it is his own insignificance... The tragedy of his inability to find himself is complete..." (from an article by Alexei Grigoriev on Heidegger).

Monday, November 2, 2009
Auditions were held yesterday. The day proved difficult. None of the actors seemed to be what we were looking for... Some incomprehensible mistakes were made. For the part of Sergei, for instance, Elina brought us a 45 years old actor for some reason. The other candidates presented to us were not encouraging either. We went into our room (in the cellar) and found *2001: A Space Odyssey*. A white space, reflecting surfaces, armchairs... The sterility of it all was intimidating at first glance. Today though, it created quite a different impression. It was pleasant to be in there and the atmosphere seemed to encourage creativity. We got bogged down in working out the details for the scene in the café... Elena's motivation is not clear and becomes even less so in the course of the scene... Overnight Oleg amended it and early (!!!) the next morning he rang and read me his new version of the scene. Later in the day we adjusted (shortened) the scene between Katerina and her father...

That day Mikhail and I met up for the first time in the new space. We put the first eight episodes together by memory. Tomorrow we'll work on the episodes that come after that (Elena leaving the house, the savings bank and her journey to visit Sergei).

Alexander the location manager came by. We discussed the suggestions he had already come up with. *None* of it was what we were after. We decided to continue the search in other directions... That night Oleg turned up and read out the new version for Episode 54 and again we made some changes (unlikely to be the final ones).

Friday, November 6, 2009
Mikhail and I decided to devote the day to looking for external locations. At Alexander Voronov's suggestion we set off to Maryino, Brateyevo & Biryulyovo[18].

We found some places that were interesting. The power-station in Biryulyovo loomed up scarily over the residential blocks. The beehive-like apartment block was right colour-wise and next to it was a single-storey building (also of a dark, appropriate colour), which could be made to look like a food shop. There was a 'street' of green garages... and... an apple orchard... We took a lot of photographs... and there were plenty of things that seemed right. We felt we were getting somewhere (with the ending cracked as well). We looked at what had been photographed on the computer that evening back in the office. Good vibes...

Saturday November 7, 2009
I spent the whole day at home. The whole day. Pyotr & Anya... I started to recover and feel like my old self again...

Sunday, November 8, 2009
More auditions. We were really struck by Elena Lyadova and very glad to have found her. She's ideal for Katerina – nothing's 'missing', no 'allowances' have to be made. She fits the role completely, as if she had been moulded from the same material as Katerina. I'm afraid to tempt providence, but Lyadova (so far) heads the list. She is without doubt better than those whom we saw previously.

We were also struck by an actress called Anna (I don't remember her surname) who 'shifted' our idea of Elena (mere speculation, of course, at this stage, but an idea which seemed right for steering our thoughts about the character of Elena). This Anna was the type of woman that people might categorise as 'simple'. It even seems as if the last ten (?) years of a comfortable life are not enough to blot out her origins, which no amount of silk and cashmere can conceal. This is what we want. This is in tune with my very first thoughts about Elena... Later everything pointed, however, towards a character with

---

[18] Maryino, Brateyevo and Biryulyovo – suburban working-class neighbourhoods on the outskirts of Moscow.

more depth, one that was not so two-dimensional... In other words, the 'presence' we find in say Nadezhda Markina is completely lacking in Anna: despite Markina's simplicity and possible (indeed very possible) 'woman-of-the-people' exterior, there is another layer (or facet) to her – a certain dignity with an almost aristocratic flavour.

I would say, and I shall have to steel myself to be that bold – that I should make the *main* female role an individual fairly easy to 'understand', if I can use that word. Devoid of secrets, which are usually seen as indispensable, without any background story. She is an ordinary individual, who by some accident of fate has wormed her way into a social environment that is definitely and blatantly not her own... Nadezhda is not a bad actress, indeed definitely not, but one who needs to shed certain theatrical habits she has acquired over the years. If we can get rid of that to some extent, then there'll be something interesting and rather unfamiliar there, indeed something quite outside the common mould. *Bold* even! It would be unusual to use an actress like that for the main character in a 90-minute feature film.

"It's probably rather awkward to raise the question, but my pension is something I can dispose of with complete freedom as I see fit..."

"That's not the point... That was not what I was saying? I'm not talking about money, but your Sergei..."

"Let's not talk about it any more. After all, I don't tell you how to behave with your daughter..."

Thursday, November 19, 2009
Today I felt encouraged by my meeting with an actor from The Oleg Tabakov Theatre[19], Yevgeny (can't recall his surname). Aged 31. He was good as Sergei. He turns out to be from the same part of the country as me. When a talented individual appears, you immediately get a sense that everything's going to be all right. The text works well and everything's seems to be falling into place. It's not a question of the actual dialogue or words, but the force of the meaning. When a gifted individual appears in a scene for some reason or other, it's the talent that counts: it doesn't even matter which actual words

---

[19] The Oleg Tabakov Theatre – located in Chistiye Prudi, Moscow, and founded by Oleg Tabakov – a highly-regarded Soviet and Russian actor.

he utters. You're looking at the person and it doesn't matter which particular words burst from his mouth. He simply lives through the force behind the meaning of what he's saying and that makes him real and hence just right for the task. Lyadova produced the same effect.

Friday, November 20, 2009
At last they've signed the script contract with Oleg and I. The next one will be the director's contract. Ponkratov needs to make Vladimir's flat look properly lived in. Everything needs to look as if it's had some wear and tear, not straight from the shop. The window glass in Sergei's flat needs to be 'wavy' so that it distorts the real world beyond it. Beyond the kitchen window, for example, and possibly the one in the living room as well – even if not in all the rooms (apart from the baby's) – opposite the beehive-block... Their flat consists of only two rooms. Sasha doesn't even have his own 'space'. Just a corner of the living room, the corner with the computer.

Sunday, November 22, 2009
Nadezhda Markina arrived at last and made us all glad. Today Elena Morozova came as well and, as I thought she would, she made a good impression as well. The only thing that put me on my guard was the 'demonic' air about her. She gives out vibes which are 'hypnotic', almost dangerous. This part's hers, just right for her, made for her. I need to try her out in the scene with her father, and Lyadova too, as they're the two main contenders. My impression is that Morozova can be this character, but that she needs to spend some time inside this part, while Lyadova is Katerina already. She too is a tear-away, never at a loss for words and not afraid to say exactly what she thinks at a given moment. Morozova is looking for inspiration in Katerina's behaviour so as to play the part, although she herself is a rather 'unpredictable' individual. Lyadova's acting is straightforward, Morozova's is whimsical. It's time to choose...

Friday, November 27, 2009
Location. The lawyer's office. Near Kievskaya metro station. One of the best alternatives suggested by Voronov. All the furniture is white leather – even the surface of the table. And the room where they take tea has a glass roof and a balcony. The atmosphere is more or less

right – transparent, quiet and business-like. A little over the top, but not tasteless.

At the Artplay Design Centre. Cold, ex-factory premises converted for use as an exhibition space, for displays of various kinds of contemporary art. This could be Katerina's space. We need to think it over.

Saturday, November 28, 2009
We all managed to get out into some fresh air: Anya, Pyotr and I... The young parents took their child out into the 'world'... The child doesn't know it but that was a real treat for his parents. Anya drove and I sat with (a sleeping) Pyotr on the back seat. The day was almost like a dream. I'm not managing to get enough sleep by a long chalk. There's no time off and it doesn't look as if there's going to be any. There's no time and nowhere to build up some energy. I have less and less, chances to boost it are few and far between and prospects for making up for lost time in this respect look very doubtful. It's tough. Everything's tough at the moment...

Sunday, November 29, 2009
A bad day. Bad auditions. None of the actors are at all suitable. Everything's substandard: if not the actual acting, then their outward/external expression are wrong. The only exception is E.G. – a wonderful actress and of course she has plenty of vitality. She is in full control of her range of emotions. Yet something's not quite right. I need to take another look at her, particularly because she was the first and only candidate for the role of Elena before the idea of using Nadezhda Markina cropped up. I need to have another look at E.G., but there's something off which I can't put into words.

We haven't really got things off the ground yet, but all of a sudden there's a sense that things are going to collapse. I have a very unpleasant feeling that some major mistake's been made. Perhaps that is the case, perhaps that's how it ought to be, particularly when we're just starting out...

It's difficult to explain the motivation behind some of the actions of certain characters. When you start digging about for motives behind this or that action or twists in the plot, all you end up with are questions. I don't know whether that's a good thing. I feel as if sing my grip on the whole thing, as if the whole is breaking into parate components, which it will be difficult to join up again. There's something frightening happening to the whole plan. Some scattered pieces – more or less successful on their own – occasionally come to the surface (like photographs being developed in the dark room) but won't join up with each other. There's nothing to hold them together, no cement, no core which would make of all the parts a whole. Only occasionally, very rarely, do I get the feeling that all of these are just temporary problems and that soon everything will come out all right and that there will be a sense of the whole, that it will all hang together. Feelings like that are rare rays of sunlight in an overcast week.

I'm worried lest panic should get hold of me, I need to put all that behind me and move forward. What will be, will be, but for now I don't even know what I should say to the actors after auditions, where to send them, what to put right... I need support, while that's what they're looking to me for. I must put this sense of looming catastrophe behind me. Where can I gain some confidence in my own abilities? Confidence that we'll get on top of all the problems. Grim premonitions... What kind are they? It's irrational, but there must be some explanation for it all... I need to get to the bottom of this mood and then discard it as something unnecessary.

Vladimir is the face of capital, a phenomenon which is dying and on the way out. The source of parasites, of protest and poverty. Nature herself is destroying him. Nature as mother. Progenitrix of that very same poverty, the other side of consumer society... Migrant workers. The face of a migrant worker. Barbarian Invasions. A good title if it hadn't been used for that splendid film by Denis Arcand. A watershed. Invasion... Locusts... Switzerland has officially banned minarets. Capital will be obliged to change the paradigm in some way. Things cannot just go on and on like this. There's bound to be some kind of change. Nature will win out. Elemental forces or Chaos... Back to the apes. Darwin will turn in his grave. Degradation and change in the human species. Nature (Mother) is changing her appearance, her essence. (Unconsciously) Nature supports the instinct for survival. All values (moral ones) are in doubt. Values are being re-examined. The Great Re-appraisal of values. Like the Great Migration of the Peoples. A mere hundred years ago, at the beginning of the 20th century there were more than 2 billion people on earth. Over the last hundred years the size of the Earth's population has more than tripled... There is no geometrical progression yet as in the information sphere, but there has been a Great Leap into nowhere... Resources are running out. Reserves of clean fresh water... etc. Over this period Capital has turned man from *Homo sapiens* into a consumer, but this process is impossible to sustain indefinitely. There is bound to be a malfunction if there hasn't been one already. Great civilisations were often razed to the ground, reduced to ashes by tribes of barbarians. Barbarians are possessed of strength, enormous primordial strength. Ignorance, thirst, hunger and the lack of those taboos, which might subject men to a process of civilisation.

Vladimir/Elena – old values, drawn from the past. Strict judgements, clear thinking, sensible strategies combined with love, gentleness, maternal concern and (a little) superstition (idol-worship). Progress via reason/tradition towards feelings.

Katerina/Sergei/Tatiana – the new generation of today (or at least a part of it) with its own values: it is impossible to say whether its parasitic ideology has been deliberately chosen or not, but it seems to have evolved among these members of that generation.

And then: Sasha/Viktor – the future... Surveyed from this angle, what is uppermost is degradation... Was it always like that or is this the sign of a new era? Or is this an overly biased view of reality?

(It's possible that Tatiana should be given a different name and be called Barbara).

Awareness of degradation is the key to progress (as a process and not 'progress' in the usual sense of the word)...

The paternal civilisation in our country is undergoing a crisis: the female, maternal, material, matter is emerging on the surface from its once suppressed and 'humiliated' state and extracting (rescuing) itself from hopelessness and shifting to the sphere of the primitive, chaos, instincts...

This process is not a rational one (generally speaking what is rational is paternal, structured, reasonable, deliberate etc.) but elemental, just as any mother will save her child not taking anything else into consideration, any arguments based on what is reasonable... She saves what is hers, she saves a real person...

On the subject of Ponkratov. Everyone must concentrate on their own work and not poke their nose into other people's domains. There's a fine example of this from the work of creative artists. I heard about this somewhere and it made a strong impression: a painter who has been studying colour, its shades and what happens to colour when paints are mixed, ceases to see (to perceive) volume. A sculptor who has been moulding clay or hewing stone all his life gradually ceases to see colour... I know nothing about what an artist's craft involves with its nuances, ways of doing things and all those magentas and cornflower blues, additions of 'warm tones' or why ochre might not be necessary in a particular place... I can only voice an opinion on what I'm presented with and say, "Yes, that's very good"; "That's more or less what's needed" or simply "That's precisely what we need", but I would never dream of interfering in what goes on in the workshop, in the inner workings of the artistic process. Everyone should concern himself with his own sphere.

The judgments that I'm hearing all around me: "There's no positive character", "There's no-one I can sympathise with", "Why is everything so hopeless, where is the light at the end of the tunnel?", "Where's the positive hero?", and so on are all rooted in tradition. What we have is some mildewed view of the subject, of the development of dramatic material. These are judgements of a philistine (in the best meaning of that unpleasant word), like the painter's judgement of the three-dimensional, while he himself is engrossed in the play of colour on a surface, or the sculptor's judgement of patches of colour and the correlation between them, when what has loomed up before his gaze throughout his life has been white marble.

Try and talk about the humanities and questions of philosophy with sportsmen, with people who have spent their whole lives training. They will happily talk to you about calf muscles or questions of concerning tendons, because – if for no other reason – they know everything about those, but avoid really abstract subjects. And that's a normal state of affairs. Not every artist is a Michelangelo – a sculptor and painter in a single individual. That's an experiment, which naturally involves some risk... But that's my right – to make mistakes, to use unusual materials for sculpture. No heroes, no Happy End. No hope. "Everything will be fine..." Haven't we had a bellyful of that mantra by now? Outside tradition, in spite of tradition. Without those revolting 'positive heroes', without the usual rhetoric, without that phoney 'empathising' but with 'shared thinking', not starting out from the familiar but sculpture based on new principles, using unfamiliar material. Something new, different, risk-laden... On the brink of disaster. We shouldn't get caught up in what other people are doing, in what's going on around us. We should move to the edge and not remain safely in the middle, jammed up against the others, like sardines in a can.

Monday, December 7, 2009
It's snowing. The roads are in chaos. Everything's come to a standstill. It took me two hours to get home this evening. I'd have done better to take the Metro. Today has been the first day of snow in Moscow. I've divided the whole script up into 14 chapters.

At this point we've been through the script from the beginning to the end of Chapter 2. (1) is the Introduction and (2) 'Elena's Journey'. Here she is already in Sergei's flat. I need to think through the space of Sergei's flat, to make sure the staging there is going to be easy. Sorting out that space is tied in with sorting out the visuals and the rhythm for the scenes in that flat (and not only the immediate ones but also those which come afterwards in the ending). In other words when we sit down to work on Sergei's space we have to include the interiors for the 'entrance hall' and the 'landing'. Things are moving slowly. On the other hand some of the scenes from later on have already been planned in detail. For instance, the 'Heart Attack' chapter (almost in its entirety). Also virtually all the episodes in the Fitness Centre, while the chapter 'Vladimir's Journey' is almost complete as well.

So I don't think we really need to worry about the pace we're gradually building up. Somehow things are falling into place little by little. The breakdown of the script into chapters now looks like this:

- Introduction.
- Elena's Journey.
- At Sergei's Home. Money for Sasha.
- Request.
- Vladimir's Journey.
- Heart Attack.
- Hospital.

- Announcement of the Will.
- Plan.
- Execution.
- Morning without Vladimir.
- Elena's Second Journey. Lawyer. Omen.
- At the Sergei's home. End of the World.
- Epilogue.

As before I'm worried about the actors. We haven't got a Vladimir yet. There isn't an actor about whom I could say: "Yes, perhaps...". Another Sergei turned up on Thursday though. And I even feel that he's still more interesting than Yevgeny (Miller) from The Tabakov Theatre. Miller is very good but he comes over as a 'shifty', rather street-wise fellow, very sprightly. The other one's on the sly side, but down-to-earth and would appear to have been born in the kind of places that Sergei inhabits. As for his 'exterior' – it's just what's needed.

Thursday, December 10, 2009
Once again the actors are not right, they don't fit. I've had enough of nannying these 'unpredictable creatures'. It's time to call in some *actors*... To hell with it all. Enough is enough, Elina...

Friday, December 11, 2009
Are we shooting live cinema or not? This is a question that came out of the blue: is this artificial, suspended, invented – or something real, or at least an approximation of reality? Mimesis. Recognisable at the level of 'memory' of life experiences. According to Plato, mimesis ('recognition' or 'reflection of life') is the imitation of the external aspect of objects, the simple copying of appearances, which – in his opinion – will not lead to truth... Yet nowadays, more than two thousand years after those ideas were born and as many centuries of their triumphs, how can we not regard them as the only correct ones – recognition and imitation of life? The elaboration of the inner essence, which goes beyond the confines of simple recognition – concentration or hyperbole within the framework reflecting life, but carrying within itself all that inner content. As the popular saying goes, the river 'has swollen' when the ice starts to melt in the spring. This should be accomplished not through acting, that should always

be modest and keep within its framework, but by different means: for example, generalisations, mysteries or leaving things unspoken. As for example, when we can imagine Sergei with all sorts of occupations. Or when we ourselves decide what the motives must have been which determined a certain decision to act made by a character. Or when something appears to have been 'left out', leaving us (the audience) to fill the lacuna with meaning. Techniques like that would appear to enable us to 'whisk' reality to the desired 'texture'. On top of everything else this 'texture', the additional component provided by the individual experience of the film-goer, broadens the space of the film and perhaps brings it nearer to spectators, even frighteningly near. This is a key question. It needs to be resolved within a mere 3 months... What a joke....[...]

Tambourine, Drum[20] – the concept behind this film was good and there were excellent seeds of ideas, but somehow it did not all hang together. [...] At the end you sense a false note. No, not the actual ending – the lad on the empty road among empty fields – that moment is a magical one, but rather all the 'blood'. Why did he have to insist on that "loss of blood" by all the characters? Utterly tasteless that bloody outcome. What for? She got up from her chair with bloodstains under her raincoat intimating loss of life (for some reason even a rhyme from Cyrano appears out of the blue) and that was that. The ending in the empty field. Full-stop. It was a pity. Everything was fine at the beginning. I'll await Mizgiryov's next film with interest. He's developing. He's going places. One of a rare few – independent, tenacious and highly talented.

Thursday, December 17, 2009
Pyotr's two months old. He's a good lad, too good. Our blue-eyed grunter.

Today I met up with Mikhail late. He only turned up at half past three. The day before his diesel-powered car had frozen up and he had spent half today unfreezing it. It took us a long time to get down to real work. We got as far as the hospital chapter, but no further than its first episode, where Elena comes out of Vladimir's ward in tears. There are still various shots of her continuing on her way afterwards

---

[20] *Tambourine, Drum* (2009) – a film made by the scriptwriter and director, Aleksei Mizgiryov.

which we have not finalised, not to mention all the editing work. An idea suddenly occurred to us for a new way to shoot his 'collapse' in the water. In other words the girl, who jumps in the water to rescue the 'man', may turn out to be unnecessary as well. Vladimir gets into the pool, starts swimming up and down a lane and that's all... Then we move straight to Elena in the flat doing her cleaning, when there's a telephone call... and the next shot is the hospital. Elena is walking quickly down the corridor. The actors we saw today were nothing special, although Yevtifiev wasn't at all bad. He's rather old, of course, and doesn't drive a car, but there's still a spark in him, I'd even say of a highly appropriate kind. He discussed the situation between Vladimir and Elena in an honest, meaningful and even cynical way... He was right for the role in many respects. He had some very apt things to say about the part, the situation and Vladimir's relationship with Elena and his daughter... Not bad at all the way he ran through the scene. Not bad at all... I'm looking forward to tomorrow's audition. Looking forward to it optimistically!!! An actor from Kiev – Sergei Romanyuk. Markina will be there as well. And Morozova will be coming... It'll be a good day. I also need to have a photo taken for my US visa and see to some private matters, otherwise things that need sorting out at home just pile up and don't get done... Tomorrow's going to be a day and a half. Soon, in the next few days, Porokhovshchikov will be arriving. I'm looking forward to that as well.

Saturday, December 26, 2009
We got acquainted with Vladislav Kirpichov. Inga and I came to the exhibition organised by EDAS[21] and were introduced to him so that we might acquaint ourselves with the principles underlying the teaching that goes on in his studio. Inga started objecting strongly, maintaining that education (particularly for young children) should lend structure to their lives, be based on some kind of framework: clear precise ideas, which will mould a 'firm' understanding of the world. In other words 2x2=4. She was saying that for a really young child (aged four, for instance) there is a big risk that you may set free his consciousness too early, before it has had time to take shape properly or absorb any basic rational ideas, and that too much of a

---

[21] Vladislav Kirpichov's EDAS studio (Experimental Children's Architecture Studio).

free rein can leave room for the irrational to seep in... It was total nonsense in my opinion...

As for the project... There was a sour aura about it all, somehow. Very sour. Maybe those are just my worries. Something about emotional burn-out, when all cats are grey and nothing can cheer you up any more. One could also mention the glass, which is half-empty...

Tuesday, December 29, 2009
I had a tooth out in the morning. A molar. Quite an undertaking... In the afternoon I cancelled a meeting with Vitorgan[22], because I was incapable of speech.

Sunday, January 17, 2010
Pyotr is three months old. A big lad already. He's talking...

I watched the film *Tulip*[23]. Magnificent film!

Petersburg. Actor auditions... I was horribly ill during the first two weeks. I felt completely trapped. A virus. The whole family caught it. Even Pyotr came down.

Wednesday, January 20, 2010
"Men marry because they are tired and women because they are curious" – Oscar Wilde.

Monday, January 25, 2010
Evil incarnate on the idiot-box. This constant barrage of intellectually degrading fodder! The national stations here operate like the couple in *Natural Born Killers* who defeat everybody around them because there is a taboo or sort of social/moral ban on certain actions and society does not expect that this 'ban' will be disregarded just like that, without any warning signal. But these guys don't play by the rules – this is not what these channels have agreed on. Revolution for the scum, hollow mediocrity. Ratings at *any* price. A person who is now standing on the side of destruction (as if it was the end of time) and is bent on the total ruin of the edifice (which was already

---

[22] Emanuel Vitorgan – a famous theatre and cinema Soviet actor.

[23] *Tulip* (2008) – a film directed by Sergei Dvortsevoi.

rickety) will not experience any difficulties. It is easy to destroy the edifice, because it was cobbled together partly from illusions or, to put it more clearly, from Utopias, but you should not attempt this. As usual this 'work' is carried out by a rough-and-ready structure calling itself authenticity, truth. *Truth* of this kind has little value. It is extremely easy to engender, because it is based on instinct, on the simplest of coarse matter.

A delusion, that's what it is – the real value of this "renaissance of Russian cinema". [...] This 'menses' run wild – this Lilith of a dying society, in which connections are disintegrating... The evil incarnate of our age. And one of the demons steering this infernal force is of course Ernst, the head of Channel One Russia. The oracle in every flat, the intimate friend and comrade of all those at home, bearing with it sweet poison mixed with nonsense... By the way it's perfectly human, in fact too human [...] The world is being destroyed. Possibly it ought to be destroyed. But heaven forbid that you should wreak that destruction. Preserving it is probably not one of the finest parts to play either, because that is a role for the doomed. The 'world' will be destroyed. [...] What will there be in its place? I'm not talking morality here. I'm not a puritan, nor a hypocrite. We ought to speak the *truth*, but is that really it? No, not that petty truth that drags us down, nor the truth that 'elevates' us and draws us up towards the pathos of humanist 'heights'. Neither one nor the other – they are both too extreme... Truth that reveals the core of an average human being is perhaps what I'm after. Shedding light on the complete mystery and unpredictable nature of the motives and reasons why an individual acts as he does. Shedding light on an absolute truth – that is what it is meaningful to investigate. Not humanism, nor romanticism, nor post-modern cynicism – man is not an insect or an angel, indeed what is he? Man pure and simple – no more, no less. And what will the film *Elena* be? A similar search? Yes, perhaps. *For truth*... But from a different angle, from a different source. I very much hope so. [...]

What will happen with this film of ours? Will a monster or a beautiful creature be born? It's a mystery and more exciting than any that have gone before. This state of uncertainty, this lack of clarity full of anxiety and confusion is appealing to me more and more. This dangerous path is engrossing and appears like an interesting adventure (journey)... We shall wait and see.

* *Moscow – Los Angeles/Aeroflot*
The point where all the ideas intersected – the obvious ones and those only anticipated, which led me to take up this film – was that point where present-day reality meets the figure of Dostoevsky's merchant's wife lighting a candle in church. The philistine as the most horrific phenomenon (the terrible lot of human existence). It is I think the Devil in the Brothers Karamazov who says: "My dream is to turn into a plump merchant's wife, who lights a candle for the dead in church and perhaps for the health of her little relatives as well...".

Or there is also Svidrigailov's [24] idea of paradise – I need to remember it and find it... Paradise is compared to a bath-house with spiders in it... Very much our Russian kind of Paradise... and there's Elena as something unshakeable, indestructible, an 'anchor for life', that is ugly and indescribable. The devil in a skirt... The merchant's wife, who justifies *everything* in the name of furthering material life.

Sundance. I had been sure that 'Sundance' was the name of a town, but it turns out that 'Sundance' is only the name of the festival. The town in which it takes place is called Park City.

Elena. I need to find a key to the central (culminating) scene. What is it? A drama? Or a tragedy? The character's mode of existence. If it's a drama then it is a reflection and there would then need to be a duality in Elena. A hidden layer. 'Doubt' if one can call it that. if it's a tragedy then there is no second plan. She (Elena) is there in her entirety, in the whole fullness of her being epitomised in her decision. After taking the decision to kill Vladimir she acts in a single-minded way, without any doubts (the mere hint of her resolve must be terrifying, because it is resolve without hesitation). She is prey to trepidation, not real fear (it is not fear!) but rather a sense of solemnity. The ritual nature of what is happening. What is terrible for us is that we are looking into the face of frightening impassivity. We are confronted by a Monster. In the beginning we see a model of caring femininity, maternal kindness and gentleness and then – a beast of prey: the moment when an individual's inner core is revealed, her physical origins – animal origins. It is not a time for re-appraising values but

---

[24] Svidrigailov – a character from Dostoyevsky's novel *Crime and Punishment*, a passionate and a criminal man, a rival and a friend of the 'Christ-like' Prince Myshkin.

for ignoring them, as if useless crumbs were being swept off a table. Barbaric times... The key value is *money*. Everything is for the sake of money and there are no restraints (moral laws, morality, conscience, humanity and so on) – just one goal – enabling oneself and one's tribe to survive. Blood ties. Barbaric times. Nature overcomes morality, reason, moral laws. In the chaos, the troubled times, matter and Nature win out...

Matter (the maternal, the senses) gains the upper hand over against metaphysics (the paternal, the rational, reason).

In general, what I want to achieve in this film is 'lightness'. Lightness with regard to the narrative and the actors' mode of existence. The dialogue must flow freely, words must come to the actors easily: there must be no 'Russian acting' – nothing heavy, significant, weighed down with pauses. Usually this is something difficult to achieve with Russian actors - their habits and practices set my teeth on edge.

I'm still not well. I've been ill, damn it, for almost a month. I would never have thought that I would be out of the saddle for that long. My brain is simply not coping with the build-up of questions which need resolving without delay. Plus it's under the weather too: my head feels heavy – it does not feel clear and transparent. Nor does my body have any light springiness in it. I fell ill (took to my bed) back on January 6th and am still – almost a month later – in a permanent state of feeling neither here nor there. The trip to Petersburg didn't help either, of course. I should have put off that expedition or have cancelled it altogether (Who was to know that it would not reap *any* results?). Without getting back on my feet I flew first to Petersburg and then back to Moscow and five days after that off to America. That's why what I didn't get rid of and flush out of my system is still inside me, very much alive. I can't see my way through this mist. I feel like just 'handing myself into' a clinic – "Take me in and cure me however you want, but get me back on my feet (and, moreover, without delay), back to full health." Perhaps I shall do that...

Actors, all I can see are actors! How difficult it is to find what you're looking for!

We do seem to be getting some kind of ensemble together. There is a feeling that things are starting to fall into place. It's encouraging to feel that the 5-6 characters, including Sasha, are all cut from one and the same cloth. They're all from the same breed, you could say. The way they go about their acting is in the same kind of key.

This is very cheering. Very. What's left is sorting out the lawyer and the two doctors: the doctor in the hospital and the doctor from the ambulance service. I haven't got actors for those parts yet. Igor Sergeyev might suit for the latter role (specifically that one, rather than the doctor in the clinic, I think). The lawyer – man or woman? What about: a man (of means) has died and now 'three damsels' are sitting over his 'legacy' and sharing it out like three beasts of prey. We need to think about that way of doing it.

I'm getting better. The sooner the better.

Wednesday, January 27, 2010
NHK (the Japan Broadcasting Corporation) has established an award for best script. Script-writers from four continents (or rather regions) will compete for the right to be acclaimed the best. The first round involves the selection of the three best scripts from each region – Latin America, North America, Europe and Japan. This means that 12 scripts make it to the final. Then the total is reduced to four – one from each region.

At the Sundance Festival they have now announced the winners. We are among them. That in itself is pleasant but, most important of all, it means prestige for the film itself, i.e. thanks to this event (our winning), it will be much easier to find distributors and possible co-producers world-wide. It has become apparent that the Sundance Institute logo is highly prestigious on the global scene. A representative of the company Sony Classics expressed interest on the very next day in meeting me and – most important of all – in discussing questions connected with possible collaboration. It was not just a question of co-producing *Elena* (or of distribution rights) but also about possibly financing a major project (up to $10,000,000, which is the sum they might put up for co-financing a film!). If that were to happen, it would be wonderful. But I am afraid it's only words so far. We'll see. I want to send them 'Grapes'. You never know...

The money which NHK pays out for the future budget of the winners' films is not spectacular – $85,000, but, as I said before, the money's not the most important thing. As I realised later on (i.e. only when I got here to Sundance), if a project has not yet got off the ground, here in Sundance it might be possible to find the finance needed for a film. The producers have flown in for the Award Ceremony.

Sunday, January 31, 2010
My last day in Park City. It's a fine sunny little town (a mining community it turns out). For a long time now mines and gold-digging have only lived on as legend. What people are using in the town at the moment are skis. Sundance is now the main festival in the world for independent cinema. I've had a good time here with Vanya, who Rodnyansky provided as my interpreter. Vanya is an intelligent fellow, young and – possibly for that reason – an extremely optimistic individual with a positive outlook. The two of us are going to fly to LA where I'm due to audition Yevgeny Nikolaevich Lazarev.

Thursday, February 4, 2010
The audition with Lazarev is over. Many unexpected things happened in the process. First of all I ran out of film, because I had ruined some back in Park City. I wound it back leaving 20 minutes' worth and then some white bands started cutting across the images. The cameraman asked for a cleaner cassette. The next day (we had decided for several artistic reasons to extend the audition) the battery died on us and in order to re-charge it we needed a Europe/America adaptor. I had to go into town and buy one. Then the same problems cropped up again: not enough film and the horizontal stripes across the shots, which made it difficult to look at what had been filmed. Lazarev proved very patient. He said that he was keen to go back to his 'motherland'. I tried to clarify when he actually planned to do that, since things are going well for him in America at the moment – he's in demand as an actor (and that is really the case – not so long ago he played the part of the Pope in *The Pink Panther* and very recently he appeared in *The Iron Man* and then in the role of Mickey Rourke's father and, in general, I think there'll be plenty of Russians for him to portray) and also as a teacher etc.. I tried gently to clarify once again, when he was planning to come back to Russia. Choosing his words carefully, he said: "My wife and I want to spend the last part of our old age in Moscow." I very much doubt that Yevgeny Lazarev is right for my character. There's something not quite right about him

as a candidate for the part, just as there's something not quite right about the character itself. Vladimir is not a part for Lazarev. Yet it was appropriate to have come this far to see him.

Moscow.
What are those questions about love for? "Do they love each other?" They seem naïve to me, asked by people who have probably never put that question directly or impartially to themselves. From the script it is obvious that their relationship is based on what we can call mutual advantage, i.e. a 'trade-off'. It's convenient for him because a housewife has moved in (with rights very much like those of a servant). And what's very clear is that she can only start 'standing up for herself' in jest: after Vladimir comments that the girls in the hospital are "not bad," Elena threatens – "I'll cut off your oxygen" – by way of an example. Vladimir can be totally free of any obligations towards Elena (as can be deduced from their silent understanding of what each other's role entails) with regard to any affairs on the side. She tolerates all this because she has no alternative. Both of them know this and do not refer to it. Elena has long 'reconciled herself' to this situation. That acceptance is of a specific kind: she understands and accepts her place in his life. She has been dependent on him right from the start: what attracted her to Vladimir was that he would be setting her free from unrelenting poverty, the constant need to 'make ends meet'. What's more, the very fact that Elena hands over her whole pension every month to her son and has been doing so for several years demonstrates that Vladimir is to some extent right when he says that he's supporting Elena's family. The relationship is a mutually convenient one, but they refer to it as 'love'.

It does not mean that it is precisely because of this that the subsequent events ensue, i.e. it is not the reason for what Elena carries out, but (I'm sorry to have to say it) that's how we live... All of us... Or almost all of us... And we see our life as enveloped in love... A terrible story. Terrible in its truth...

Sunday, February 28, 2010
Today (Sunday) the final decisions on the actors were due to be

announced. We had all assembled: myself, Elina, Alexander Badion[25] and Mikhail. Something was wrong even at that stage. One of those present should not have been there. There was terrible tension in the air almost all the time, i.e. for several hours. We looked through the material.

Today there was an unbearable amount of takes and versions of scenes with Elena. I had lost all interest in what was being shown on screen. There should have been a single take for each of the three actresses and that was all (and also the episodes with Katerina).

The atmosphere was tense, I didn't want to watch anything or see anyone. Yet I had to get a grip on myself and then light a cigar – an essential accessory for the occasion – and announce the decision for the three (only three!) main characters: Elena, Vladimir and Sergei. In addition to them – so as to fulfil the obligation I had taken on myself of "confirming four parts today" – I also announced our decision regarding the woman at the towel-counter (in the fitness centre). Elina contacted Markina and gave her what I hope were glad tidings. She also told Rozin that he had been given the part of Sergei. Then came the main event of the day. It was decided that I should tell Andrey Smirnov about his having been given the part. I telephoned and then suddenly *(suddenly!!!)* heard a refusal. He told me in a very emotional voice that disaster had struck his own film[26], that he would not have time to finish the editing (to redo the editing in order to shorten it) not just by March (tomorrow is already March 1st) as he had planned in November, but even by June...

"I'm sitting on a powder keg: if I do not manage to complete this work, it will be a disaster..." etc. How could he possibly start working with us in April and May, if there had been such a disaster with his own film?... etc. We wound up the conversation and he said that, in general, that was his final answer and there could not be an appeal. I put down the receiver with a feeling of horror... One catastrophe had set in motion another. What was to be done? It was awful...

---

[25] Alexander Badion – the cameraman making a film about *Elena* and videos of the actors' auditions.

[26] At that time Andrey Smirnov was editing his own film *There Once Lived a Simple Woman*.

March 1
In the morning we discussed what could be done about this disaster. We decided on a compromise solution. We would delay the main shoot (in the studios and two interiors: the hospital and the fitness centre) till June. In April we would ask Smirnov to give us just 1-2 days for the exterior episodes. First we had to run that decision past him and then after that put it to Rodnyansky.

In the evening I rang Smirnov feeling very agitated and to my delight he did not cut me short with the word '*no*' or resort to any phrases making it clear his decision had been irrevocable. He agreed to meet me and to discuss various possibilities further...

Before that Mikhail and I had watched the rest of the film *Inglourious Basterds* in the afternoon. Mikhail condemned it out of hand: "It leaves a horrible taste in your mouth." After watching that, he did not have the slightest urge to get back to work. That was his reaction to the film. I had responded in a similar way to *Kill Bill*.

Wednesday, March 3, 2010
Today was a watershed for the project. A wonderful day, full of events. Smirnov agreed to take part. Hurrah!!!

I got up early this morning. I had to leave home by 9:00 so as to be at Smirnov's flat by 10 o'clock. To my surprise it was not difficult to get up at 8:00 and I was not late for the meeting. I had bought a bottle of good Calvados the evening before. The gift was accorded due praise and we even drank two glasses each. We had a good talk. About many different things – the problems he was having with his film: it was getting out of hand but it was a 'pity' to discard material – in other words, the usual ups and downs. At present there are $3^{1/2}$ hours of it and he has to cut it down to no more than $2^{1/2}$ at the most. He had to cut it by an hour: from what he was saying the material had been shot without without much coverage (i.e. details and cut-aways) and now it was virtually impossible to edit it, to cut down its length by getting rid of extra angles or details and so the rhythm of the action which had taken shape would be lost. By his own admission there was a good deal of monotonous material that was heavy-going and drawn out, but which could not be cut because of the way the film as a whole had been shot. We reminisced about Bergman – he and Smirnov had even been friends at some point. Smirnov told me that he had once asked Bergman which of his films meant the most to him and, after thinking it over a little, he'd said *Fanny and Alexander.* We talked in detail about delaying the shooting of his episodes till mid-May (from the 15th onwards). In general we spent a pleasant time together and had breakfast over coffee and a glass of Calvados – four of us: with his wife Lena and son Alexei. I realised that Andrey's wife and son were potential allies. They were trying to convince Andrey that he should not turn the part down. We seemed to have settled everything.

The next point on my list was Molochny Lane and a meeting with the security (consisting of two individuals) of an important citizen. Both of them soon grasped what I was after and the three of us discussed in detail all the camera angles required, all the movements involved: the car (used for the film) driving in and out, people walking in and out and so on. We were given approval for our work in Molochny Lane, which was very encouraging... The morning was heartening and very busy. Then it was back to the office and settling the new shooting schedule, specially drawn up to fit in with what Smirnov could manage. We even managed to have all the other locations approved: the church, the café, the hospital, the lawyer's office and the street down which the cars would be driving. All that still needed official approval was 'Katerina's flat', the bank and the shop in the suburban neighbourhood. We even agreed on Vladimir's car – an Audi A6. The only thing I don't know yet is whether we'll use a grey or a black one. Ponkratov suggests a grey one, whereas I had envisaged a black car...

Once again (after Ekaterina had completed some other work with Ivanov[27]) we went back to the official schedule and in general it is clear that even after the sanctioned additional Day No. 36, we're still going to really need another 1 or 2 days. We decided to leave that question for the time being. In the evening we met up with the consultant Marina (a lawyer). She told us a good deal of interesting things about the inaccuracies in the dialogue with the lawyer. She nearly brought the whole of our edifice tumbling down (!). It turned out that if Vladimir and Elena had already been married for many years and say a considerable part of Vladimir's property had been

---

[27] Sergei Ivanov – First Assistant Director.

acquired comparatively recently, then the text of the will (in the form that is presented in the text of the script) would not have made any difference to the resolution for the question of the inheritance. This meant that the text of the will would have contradicted the existing law. In other words, even if the wishes of the deceased (while he was drawing up his will) had been those we suggested in the script, regardless of the text of the will, the part of the estate acquired by Vladimir in the period when Elena was already his wife, would still have been divided equally between Elena and Katerina. To put it simply Elena would have had no need to kill Vladimir, if they had already been married for many years. So it turned out that this ridiculous act on her part was that of an ignorant person who had not taken the time to examine the essentials of the situation (or to seek advice). The story would perhaps have been even more horrific in view of the absurd and ridiculous nature of the 'unnecessary sacrifice'. For the time being the solution seemed to be as follows: all the property (both movable and immovable) had been acquired by Vladimir before he married Elena, i.e. all the inheritance about which he was talking to Elena was not *joint* property, but his *own* personal property, which by law he was entitled to dispose of as he saw fit.

In the evening we looked through (for the nth time) the videos of the auditions for actors auditioning for the roles of Sasha and Tatiana. One of the Tatianas will be in the seventh month of her pregnancy in May when we plan to film the episodes involving her... That could be interesting ("Mum! We've got a surprise for you...", "If it's a boy, we'll call him Vladimir"). But there's a risk: problems that can be linked to pregnancy, all sorts of oedemas, toxemia, changes in a body and also, Heaven forbid, any sort of medical contraindications or medical intervention to 'save' the pregnancy... In short there are more minuses and risks than positive gains. In addition the second candidate is a good actress and every bit the equal of the first one. It is complicated (complicated yet again) as far as Katerina is concerned. Once more I started liking Morozova. Lyadova too is very good, but today I noticed (scrutinised) positive nuances in favour of Morozova's acting. I decided – in order to make it an even playing field – to have Lyadova do a run-through of the scene with her father and then choosing between the two will at least be fair. I'll then have two scenes with each of them and there will be more substance to the choice. It's been a long day, but a very good one, one might even say superb. Even when it comes to my physiological state I feel I'm over the worst now, both with regard to my work on *Elena* and my own state of health.

We've had some new ideas regarding 'Katerina's flat' and now it's clearer how the episode there will plan out. We're not going to use any designers or installations, but simply film it (in the Artplay Design Centre) when the film about Žižek is being shown, for which Katerina is providing the simultaneous translation...

We need to think through the details of that solution...

Thursday, March 4, 2010
I got up very early this morning: half-past seven. Then I recalled and wrote up what had happened yesterday. I sent a message to Viktoria[28] in Paris saying I want to talk to her this evening on Skype. I need to tell her that the parts have all been assigned. A difficult job. I need to let Lazarev and Kryuchkova know as well. Uffff...

Yesterday Yuri Stepanov, an actor from the Fomenkovsky Theatre was killed in the most stupid of accidents. After the performance he waved down a gipsy taxi and soon afterwards another car drove into it (the exact circumstances we do not know yet — it's possible that the 'taxi' drove into the other car). All those involved in the collision survived except Stepanov. A terrible death. Its being so avoidable is really depressing. A talented actor and still a young man. Life moves along, you make plans, start looking forward to future changes in your life, in the life of your country, put off for later various important decisions and undertakings and then that 'later' never happens. That's life for you...

We edited the film about the locusts with great difficulty[29]. S. turns out to be very unsure of himself regarding the editing system and clearly doesn't understand my language. *At all.* He appears to take my

---

[28] A stage actress, who has been living in Paris for many years and was considered for the main role of *Elena*.

[29] A two-minute fragment was put together using material from several documentary films about an onslaught of locusts complete with a sound-track. It was made specially for the episode in the hospital, when — as planned by the director — Vladimir remains alone in front of the television late in the evening after Katerina's visit. The episode was filmed but not included in the final version of the film. It can be found on the director's official website www.az-film.com in the section 'Video'.

instructions or decisions on board in a completely opposite manner to which they are intended. As I said above, he has a very poor grasp of the editing programme. I am amazed to think that he edited [...], how on earth did he do it? The speed he works at is 4 times (and that's not an exaggeration) slower and more tedious than (a) necessary and (b) possible. Our working rhythms are a total mismatch, which has started to annoy me and drive me up the wall. It took us *a whole day* (!) to edit what could have been done in 20 minutes. I'm never going to go into an editing suite with S. again!

Saturday, March 20, 2010
There was a terrible day for our project a week ago. I hope this will mark the end of our horror stories. The cost is too high. It's so unlikely and so hard to take in, but after hoping I had put my last illness completely behind me, I fell ill again. This time it was just as serious as before. Desperation came over me and my brain was absolutely incapable of thinking about anything. It's as if it was engulfed in some sticky and resounding sense of inescapable disaster that I simply couldn't shake off...

Sunday had been set aside in advance for some more auditions. The office staff was so far behind with its work that there was no end to my amazement. In the studios where we were due to work for 8 hours, if not more (the shooting was scheduled from three in the afternoon to midnight), in the studios, where 6 actors would need to change and start performing during that time in light (indoor) clothes, it was freezing cold. It was only possible to stay there wrapped up in outdoor clothes, with heads covered and preferably with scarves on as well.

This 'ice hut', in which I had to stick it out, moving between set, make-up room and the one and only electric stove (which to some extent made up for the lack of heat), this shed full of draughts, that was utterly freezing and miserable, dealt me a fatal blow. I had to take to my bed again: for the third time since work on the film had started (at an energetic pace very different from the bedrest I needed). Once again I had this oppressive sense of weakness. My throat was sore, my nose completely blocked and my head like cast iron. Stop. It's impossible to go on like this. Konstantin Lavronenko gave me the contact number for an immunologist. He examined me (by then it was Wednesday) sent off a blood sample to test my immune status and now we're waiting for the results. He also gave me the contact details of an ENT specialist, who in his turn gave me the telephone number of a certain Nadezhda Alexandrovna, who for the last four days has been my only hope.

First of all she cancelled all the medication I had been taking previously. Literally everything, even what the immunologist had prescribed. She said: "I'll take full responsibility for this," (meaning the decision to cancel the medicines and instructions). [...] In short, rejecting antibiotics and pharmaceuticals as such, she used laser treatment for the 'inner reserves of the body'. I felt a good deal better. I'm hoping to be fully recovered very soon. Hoping...

Sunday, March 21, 2010
I came across some notes I had made two years ago. This is where *Elena* first came into being.
Outline plan for 'The Mortgage':
- A young happy couple: the dawn of their love. He and her. ... Perhaps a bicycle (an old idea).
- He is 'an artist' – a painter. Talented with an eventful life. The early stages. Poverty. Accommodation – they rent a flat or perhaps only a room.
- Discussion of their living quarters. Children. A child appears. A mortgage. Detailed conversations about that including the fact that "after all parents (hers or his?) aren't going to live forever: they'll die soon and then we'll be able to sell their flat and pay off the rest of the mortgage straightaway" – and so on.
- He starts experimenting with a new method of 'painting' and begins selling his own works successfully. He refers to this method as 'lucky'. Daubs of paint. Streaks of paint and varnish, which come together randomly to form patterns (more thought needed).
- Production of this 'commodity' assumes an almost industrial scale. As far as creativity is concerned it is meaningless or even 'kitsch' but this 'product' helps not only to make ends meet but also to pay the mortgage.
- Gradually life turns into a chase after 'prosperity' (almost without their noticing it). They start thinking about education for their child and so on.

- Suddenly interest in his works starts to decline. Perhaps everyone has already acquired 'copies'? The fashion is over, or for some other reason perhaps, things start going really badly. The couple now faces a dilemma: they have no money and don't know where to get any from, but they still have to make the monthly payments... Falling behind with mortgage payments is very serious. Something is deposited with the bank for security. A great deal, if not everything, has been staked on it.
- They decide 'to cut short' the life of the parents, so that afterwards they can sell their property. (?) Possibly that is too brutal, yet perfectly realistic in our current times.
- How?..
- Their plan runs smoothly. Perhaps she'll do it on her own, but he guesses what she's up to. Ivan Karamazov and Smerdyakov. His compromise is that he'll switch from painter to house-painter; her compromise is that she'll kill one of the parents (her own [?]: mother/step-mother, father/step-father). The children provide the justification. Everything is in the name of the children.
- The house is built 'on bones'. The address where they live might be near the Church of our Saviour on the Spilled Blood[30] (?). After the funeral they borrow some money on a temporary basis for the mortgage payments and when the legally required period is over and when the lawful heirs acquired the right to use their inheritance, they sell the parents' flat.
- At the funeral the wife cries conspicuously, not in a false, cunning way but with complete sincerity.
- The couple pays the money they received for the flat into their bank and pay off the rest of the mortgage. A 'new life' begins... That's how it seems at first. Yet their hectic life chasing round in circles after prosperity does not finish there. It is hurtling towards disaster, forward to disaster.
- One of the final images: she is sitting on her exercise bike, turning the pedals. Her face is expressionless. A lifeless mask. In the name of the children – in the name of the future. All *the gloom of the present* is in the name of the future.

---

[30] A cathedral in St Petersburg built on the site where Tsar Alexander II was assassinated in 1881 and dedicated to his memory.

All those who go on and on about "light at the end of the tunnel" deliberately call "'a comforting lie' the truth, so as not to have look the real truth in the face".

Monday, March 22, 2010
A good day, full of positive decisions and events. Early in the morning there was a medical procedure and after that I went to the hospital, to the 'set' where we're going to be filming for four days. There's a good atmosphere in the hospital – people are friendly and the head-doctor is impressive. We stood in the corridor, staring at the large ward for haemodialysis patients. There were four of them in the ward. There were several of us as well: we stood there staring around, one minute at the sun (how it moves around within that space) the next at the walls and how they reflect the light. Mikhail and Pyotr (his gaffer in charge of the lighting crew) were discussing what they needed to do, while the rest of us – Ivanov, Alexander Voronov[31], Pavel[32], the manager from the film studios, Lozovskii[33] and others – walked up and down the corridor looking into the wards and discussing various other matters.

In general the space is a good one. Outside the windows there are excellent tree-trunks (with plenty of branches and twists in them). The ward itself is appropriate, clean and spacious. In general Ponkratov was absolutely right.

From there we went to Kievskaya metro station and popped into the 'lawyer's office'. Once again I felt sure that the location was just right. Perhaps even larger than necessary for three close-ups. The room was well lit. Contre-jour lighting. A good choice. I thought about how we would start the episode. The lawyer's secretary will open the scene.

After a fairly detailed conversation with Viktoria[34], Mikhail and Ponkratov, I went to the office, where Anastasia was waiting for me and, as it turned out, there were numerous questions that needed answering. Anastasia and I worked through what was for me a new document, which I want to have on set: the whole script has now been

---

[31] Alexander Voronov – Location Assistant.
[32] Pavel Gorin – Production Manager.
[33] Alexander Lozovsky – Assistant Props Master.
[34] Viktoria Kudinova – Assistant Props Master.

broken down into 103 pages of text, each with a short description of what happens in each episode. So far we have only got as far as Episode 20. I hope to continue with that and to complete the document before we start shooting.

We already tended to keep ourselves to ourselves, but now everyone seems to have crept away into his or her corner. How do people live nowadays? What do they aspire to?.. I take refuge in my creative work... What can be done if there doesn't seem to be any way out? Prowl about like a wolf, who has to be on the move to eat? How revolting that some of these people are selling real estate – an extreme example (one of them) of how the human species is changing. How blinkered they are. It's incredible. They're like machines or automatons. A perfect example of the 'waking sleep' to which Gurdjieff[35] refers. What has happened to us? This development is not something that can be reversed (the saddest part of it all). Or at any rate so it seems at present.

It was Spengler[36] I think who expressed the idea that it is useless or foolish to go against the historical process. Not even because conservatism is doomed, but because what is new is always directed towards the future and will naturally come out on top. There is nothing wise about resisting the historical process, because there is no wisdom in such a position, no view of the present moment from a wider perspective, from the point (like a bird's eye view) which brings together the backward-looking perspective and the perspective facing the future. Possibly, indeed probably, that is not a position which is wise or rational but what dignity there is in that persistent nostalgia, in that looking backwards. And courage like that of Camus' Sisyphus, the courage of his Don Juan, who knows that love is doomed but marches forward resolutely and with gladness in his heart into the abyss.

Such is the life of a hero. I know that every life is doomed, that its end will come – tomorrow perhaps, but I do not give in, I live this life

---

[35] George Gurdjieff (1866-1949) – a Russian mystic and philosopher, traveller. He studied sacred dance in Asia and Africa and brought music and movement into his philosophical teachings on the self-development of human beings. His ideas attracted many followers among the intellectuals and artists of the day and are still popular even today.

[36] Oswald Spengler (1880-1936) – a German historian and philosopher of history whose interests included mathematics, science, and art.

as if I were eternal. "I am one of those who haul the nets, when a shoal of immortality comes in...", "There is no death either at seventeen or at seventy..." Arseny Tarkovsky[37].

The film will be about those last days.

An apocalypse of a personal and individual kind: it appears to concern only Elena, but in actual fact it is the herald of events that have a far wider impact. Signs of this are scattered everywhere – they are to be observed in the atmosphere all around us.

Moscow is the new Babylon. *Koyaanisqatsi*[38] has a mood appropriate to the end of time. It would be impossible to convey that idea in this film: indeed it is not necessary – that would be too heavy-handed. In your face... Godfrey Reggio achieves it with genius. Our film is not the place for it. Emptiness once again? Absence of any mass of people. Any *mass*, or surroundings. No there are surroundings. Of an active kind. There are plenty of people, plenty of animation, but no mass. A mass would just be chaotic.

Or this has to be conveyed by different means somehow. Technical means: (special) lenses, methods of shooting, slow motion, accelerated footage, time-lapse photography: all these devices in other people's hands yield excellent results. But... they inevitably usher in (on a royal bier) the auteur. This approach will mean a good deal (so much that it cannot be avoided) of the subjective, the personal... so that facts cease to be facts and are turned into transcription or statements...

We need objective observation... Elena and the people around her. We are there watching this together with the audience. No interference. Our having filmed it is enough. That's how I see it...

My thoughts are running round in circles and my head's aching as before. Citramon is not helping. My doctor says she has a headache too – there has been an abrupt change in the atmospheric pressure. Indications of that were today's snow-storm and Oleg's latest drinking bout.

The wretch – he'd promised that he'd stay off the drink till shooting was finished. The timing couldn't be worse because there are some urgent things he has to see to – to select (immediately what's more!)

---

[37] Arseny Tarkovsky (1907 –1989) – a Soviet poet and translator. The father of influential film director Andrei Tarkovsky.

[38] *Koyaanisqatsi – Life out of Balance* (1983) – a documentary film by the American director Godfrey Reggio.

TV programmes for Elena. He's probably been watching too many wonders of Russian television and sought solace in vodka. We're going to have a tough time in the next few days. By Sunday we have to get through: horse people (!), stuntmen, finalising the bit-parts (and there's a fair number of those!), the CGI. The horse!! The horse!! Horseman of the Apocalypse. Why did I let myself in for that episode... How difficult it is to sort all that out! The Russian film industry in action. No-one will take responsibility for anything...

We just have to take pot luck, as usual.

On Sunday it's off to Biryulyovo. All the decisions about that location. The fight... What about the fight? How are rehearsals? Countless questions. Only 17 days till we start shooting!!!

The photo-session will have to be a little earlier... April 6th or 7th. That's enough, it's time for bed. The usual procedures and then sleep...

Sunday, March 28, 2010
Thank God my recovery's speeding up. I'm getting back to normal. Saturday was a good day with plenty to show for it. In the morning we went to look at the horse (or stallion) – a fine grey stallion. They got him to lie down in the snow (it was somewhere out in Skhodnya) and demonstrated how 'puppeteers' will pull at some strings to make the animal's legs move – so as to look like a dying horse's death throes. All of that was suitably depressing. Perhaps a sleeping horse would do or one that's just starting to come to? Or perhaps we should turn to Tokoyakov[39] for help. Computerised convulsions – Heaven knows – might turn out more convincing than puppeteers' strings. Once again it's far from clear what we'll be doing after April 20th!!!

Then we went to look at the Biryulyovo location. We walked all round it. There was a good deal of snow and melting water in sizeable streams in places where we had been planning for dry paths. I hope it'll dry up by April 12th.

Friday, April 2, 2010
Yesterday I went to the premiere of *How I Ended This Summer*[40]. [...]

---

[39] Dmitry Tokoyakov – Visual Effects Supervisor, he devised a number of special effects for the film *Elena*.

[40] *How I Ended This Summer* (2010) – a film by the script-writer and director Alexei Popogrebskii.

Alexei Popogrebskii's a fine fellow and intelligent. I liked the first film he made on his own, but this picture was a disappointment.

Today I looked at the work by the stuntman. The fight. It isn't very convincing so far. The beginning's all right, before you start working out what's happening, but soon after you can see that it's all a sham. It doesn't smack of a real fight so far. You can see the blows *aren't real*. That's all got to be disguised, but how?

The shoot. The first full week of shooting's over already.
Today is the 17th of April.
The first day in the hospital. The first scene with dialogue. Before that there had been shots of people walking or travelling and the fight in the garden. It even seemed to go quite well.

Thursday, April 29, 2010
A day off with the family. We invited Mama over and we had lunch at 'Starlight Diner'. We had a pleasant walk round Patriarch Ponds. It was a good day with a lot going on. We were even tired by the end of it. Little Pyotr is a source of ever more happiness. A splendid boy. In the evening we washed him in the big bath. Feeling really happy, at night I watched the material shot so far but without the sound. There are a fair number of disappointments, but that's always the case. I don't like looking at footage we have shot, but it can't be avoided. It's (almost always) on the skimpy side, unreal somehow and there's always something not quite right. Disappointments all round...

Yesterday the shooting went really well. Lyadova was most encouraging. The fine episode with Žižek is going to turn out well. God willing!!! There's a splendid shot where she is on her own on the divan by the window.

The day in the church was also first-rate. Three or even four of the five angles were excellent. The day in the hospital was difficult (that episode with the discharge just wouldn't gel). It turned out middle-of-the-road – neither one thing, nor the other... That episode is going to end up like that – just a bit of ordinary filler. That's the feeling I have...

The owner of some brand of Scotch whisky wrote in the publicity material for his merchandise: "Don't do anything, don't say anything, don't go out of your house and then no-one will criticise you." What needs adding is "but even then someone'll come along who'll say – you're a nonentity, a nobody".

Saturday, May 15, 2010
In a few days we'll start shooting on set in Vladimir's flat. A week ago we finished filming in Sergei's flat. There's a large amount of good material. Really good. I watched plenty of other material as well with the sound and with a 2.35-1 aspect ratio. Thank goodness, I needn't have worried about the discharge episode. It's all come together, which is more than I can say for the fight in the apple orchard. I'm worried about that scene. That's the first thing I'm going to edit, so that I'll be able to raise the question of re-doing it with Rodnyansky.

Some of the shorts are not the right length, as far as their rhythm is concerned.

Weak spots:
(a) method of shooting (terribly shaky images);
(b) there is no let-up in long events (I gave the next command to Sasha after the beating-up too soon). Hopefully time adjustment using computers will sort this out, or else...

It needs re-doing. It's better to limit it to 1 or 2 takes (given the slow motion) rather than getting bogged down in 5.

We need to take another look at Igor's (Sasha's) physical state. So that the actor can *get a feel* for it. To feel the heaviness of his body... hampering his movements. Weakness and a lack of co-ordination etc.

The episode in the lawyer's office is excellent. You just don't know which of the actors to look at, when all three of them are so good...

In general it is difficult to write up this diary while shooting is in progress. Even on my days off there's no time for anything extra and definitely not during working days. All in all the process is progressing smoothly. There's a sense of satisfaction with what we have done so far. Almost everything is in tune with the original concept and much of it goes even further. With extra spice...

This applies in the main to the actors who 'enlarge' – in the best sense of that word – the characters they have been called upon to play. This applies to a large extent to Markina and Smirnov. Lyadova is very good. In some scenes it's hard to take your eyes off her. It's a powerful, extremely powerful ensemble. Now I'm writing these lines when all the main scenes with dialogue are behind us. The last day with Lyadova was over a long time ago. Recently we shot one after the other the scenes 'Request for Sasha' and 'The Will'. Markina's a miracle!!! Smirnov is also excellent. Thanks to their personalities the scenes acquired astonishing nuances, which are impossible to put into words. I'm very pleased with our choice of actors. By this stage I am also at last pleased with the set. Andrey has done very well. The solution was correct and we had the right background outside the windows. Trees!!! All we still have to do is position the crows in them...

I'm very pleased with the final version of the background outside the windows of Vladimir's flat. When we were filming the episode with the 'invasion' I even altered the angle for the close-up and middle-ground shots with Sasha on the balcony. Instead of filming him en face (with the block of flats behind him) we shot him in profile against the trees. The impression created struck just the right note – looking at the bare trunks and branches outside the window in front of the balcony... I was also very happy with shot #1 and the virtual mirror-image shot at the end when Elena's family is drinking tea and then the focus and composition are redirected towards the branches. The trident of gnarled branches and the trunk – each swaying with their own particular rhythm. The idea with that rondo was pulled off remarkably well: coming into the flat and coming out again. It's very close to what I had originally envisaged. I had not thought it would be possible to achieve that on set. It's amazing but I think it is even possible to see how the life-giving sap is flowing in those trunks and branches.

The first shot is enhanced by the two crows. I like the two takes with them. In the second the crow flies into the shot and perches exactly in the middle of it, although nobody asked the crow to do that: it simply just came to rest precisely in the middle of the shot and then folded its wings, shook them out and turned its head – as required in such circumstances.

Friday, June 11, 2010
Very sadly the bulk of the shooting would seem to be over. It's all behind us, God be praised. Yet I can't shake off the annoying feeling that the episode with the fight is off the mark. The idea that the whole of that episode might have to be re-shot in the autumn won't let go of me. The summer will decide that. The editing will make it clear...

I don't remember the day of the week, June 17, 2010
I'm in Koktebel with Andrey and Turkiya[41].
It has to be said... the people living in this house are truly remarkable... The atmosphere (more often than not in the evening) round the large table, with a large – or sometimes small – group of people drinking, can at times become something almost tangible. To say that these surroundings are artistic or creative is only the half of it. Here – perhaps because there is such an abundance of creativity, virtuosity and culture as a whole – the atmosphere is sometimes so intense that it hovers on the edge of the unreachable, always about to dissolve into thin air and lose its strength, to drown in banalities and witticisms that are not really amusing. But, as a rule, this does not happen and everything comes together with all manner of coincidences, unplanned miracles and other intellectual (but not abstruse) elegance. The climate, the quiet and the peace of this place help to make all this happen.

It is precisely the risk of *the thread* of beauty holding these evenings together perhaps being lost which is the deepest of the fears that grip you. One of many (!). If we can forget that fear, then it is possible to apprehend the very fabric of life which is being woven before your eyes, when you have the good fortune to be able to contemplate almost every one of its patterns.

These people here love life and they know how to rejoice in it. Without any empty triviality they greet each day here artistically, cleverly, radiantly and wittily. And they expect a similar response from the day itself. The most astonishing thing of all is that the response is forthcoming, because they deserve it.

[...] Over the last fifteen years the resort of Koktebel has – with each passing year – been rapidly turning into a revolting anthill. As I have been able to observe, the hordes of people in the public areas and along the shore, for example, are enough to make you feel you are pushing your way through a lively market to reach its stalls. The 'lovely' beach music - either schmaltzy 'chansons' or 'doof doof' dance beats creates an inescapable environment that seems attractive to the average Russian. But it's enough to drive a man crazy. The

---

[41] Andrey Dementiev – a film-critic, producer-in-chief for film-broadcasts for the Russian TV channel, RenTV (1996-2006); Natasha Turkiya – an artist and Dementiev's wife.

main tourist route along the beaches in the town of Sochi has the same effect. Pure horror.

Yet the rare enjoyable places in Koktebel still retain their former charm. A faint echo of what they used to be, but has been retained. Andrey's house is not on the tourist trail, which is important. So we were wrapped in peace and quiet.

Friday, June 18, 2010
Shostakovich's *Eleventh Symphony. Part Two* [?]. Grandiose power permeates the whole performance conducted by Kondrashov (Kondratov?). Incredible impact!!! That was the inspiration for the film *'Grapes'*.

The beginning and the ending of *Elena* have virtually assumed their final shape. It's important to be *bold* in my decisions. They must be bold ones. Not in a forced or over-cerebral way, not starting out from an intention 'to take a bold decision' but to be sure not to worry if a dilemma needs to be resolved in a way that might appear to you as fraught with risk. Listen to yourself, trust your intuition. Without hesitation, focus on what wells up inside you demanding expression.

This morning the film suddenly started to take definitive shape in my mind. I can see the sequence, feel its rhythm.

August 5, 2010
When I returned to Moscow after Koktebel, I started work on the editing on June 22nd. Altogether it took Anna[42] and myself 26 days and we completed the first cut on July 23rd. That same day I flew off to the sun, where I flopped like a vegetable onto a wonderful pebble beach of the Aegean with Anya and Pyotr. For the first time I was able to spend so much real time with my son in the nine months since his birth. What a wonderful boy he is. I don't understand what the state of the film is at this moment. I'm still too involved with it. There's no way I can judge it objectively. I need time. Yet watching it the day before I left gave me food for thought and made me realise that the film has to be shortened. That's something that has to be done. I already know precisely what needs to be taken out. Almost all of the

---

[42] Anna Mass – Film Editor.

later additions to the script... That was material extending the text of the film but diluting the concentration of the narrative. All that needs to be taken out to make the story simpler. That is an important requirement for the film *Elena*. Precisely for a film of this kind.

I've been reading the first version of the script for *Elena*. I've also taken a look at my earlier notes. For instance the document entitled 'Director's Angle'... A phrase there about the rhythm of the film took me by surprise. I had envisaged it as 'rapid', i.e. a year earlier the rhythm of the narrative had appeared to me rather differently. So it follows that the rhythm, dictates itself. While we were shooting and I was concentrating on the set and what the actors were doing, I could not allow myself to speed up somehow artificially the flywheel of their actions, of the dialogues and events. It had seemed to me that everything was moving at a perfectly natural pace. Did I need to suppress in myself the immediate, spontaneous urge in favour of that initial conceptual approach? Should I aspire to the outline that had presented itself to me earlier? I don't think so. A concept is one thing. Observing a fact that is unfolding before your eyes is something quite different.

THE CAMERA'S GAZE. MIKHAIL KRICHMAN

THE CAMERA'S GAZE[43]

1. A Motivated Camera

...A camera is something more than me, more than the cameraman: it can see and do more than I can. I can study it and learn to understand its actual nature. A camera is a strange beast – slow, intelligent, precise and able to gaze at a single point as if bewitched. You have to know not just how to attract its attention but how to steer that attention. If there is no reason to do so, it will not move, but simply look at what is in front of it. It might 'breathe' a little, 'help' a little, provide more air or, on the other hand, it might add pressure or tension – it has the ability... Yet it cannot move if not led somewhere by an actor, a flight of birds or the wind – by something...

Mise-en-scène moves the camera. The outer 'texture' of the action in *Elena* is full of 'injections', 'incentives' and 'summons' to the camera. In the scene, for instance, when Sergei tries to erect a 'partition wall' in the deceased Vladimir's flat and then walks 15 metres from the study as far as the fridge. For the actor to walk even a few paces, he has to make a real effort. It is not a question of the quality of his acting: what is involved is the inner nature of this particular character, the context of that particular scene. What is required of the actor is that he should cover an enormous distance, it means crossing virtually the whole of the set. If Sergei merely walks its length, then he will soon be off-camera. The camera will not

---

[43] This text is based on an interview given by Mikhail Krichman to Ksenia Golubovich and recorded in August/September 2012. Alyona Gromova, a specialist in visual communication, also took part in those conversations. The material was later reworked into a single, separate text, still containing some of the comments from the two women. They are singled out in italics.

follow him – why? It's of no interest to the camera. Then Andrey had the idea of making him turn round and ask Elena: "Is there any beer?" Then there was a motive straightaway: Sergei attracted attention and we realised that he was moving in a clearly defined direction, for a reason, and the remaining five or six steps towards the fridge were justified as far as the camera was concerned. It turned because it was faced by an interesting question: how would he open someone else's fridge, in someone else's home and drink someone else's beer?

Then again – after switching scenes very fast – we are in the railway carriage: Elena's hands are clutching the handbag containing the money. I remember precisely that we had wanted to start the shot with them. They are working hands which make Vladimir's bed, prepare his food, extract his fruit-juice, manage to mix deadly tablets in with his medication and now at last they are here clutching money. Then we needed to raise our gaze to her face and from there to the view outside the window, where a dead white horse was lying, to that 'Horseman of the Apocalypse'. Symbolically speaking, the whole of that scene was a transition from the Elena, still wracked by doubt, running, to the one who personally sets fire to the unfinished will, to the new Elena in charge of her own life and a criminal. This was the being we would see when we looked into her face the next time. How would we achieve that? What reason would there be for us, with the camera, to raise our gaze from hands to face?

Then suddenly the train shudders and starts to move. With an involuntary movement the hands grip the bag more tightly than ever. It is that movement of the hands and their nervous clutching at the bag which give the camera a chance and a *reason* to 'move upwards' to look at *her*, the woman who clutches at her riches so greedily.

Motivation for the camera is a subtle and skilled undertaking. It begins with the work of the art director and the costume designer who think through the texture of the space and costumes, inhabited by the characters. In this respect we are an indivisible whole. There are no separate individuals in the cinema. Negin, who wrote the script, knew that Zvyagintsev would shoot the film. After that they were working on it together. Later on the art director and I became part of the process and we also knew that we were making a film, specifically the work of Andrey Zvyagintsev and no other director. The director of photography and the art department are a team which cannot be divided into its separate parts. At the preliminary stage we would always start out from the characters and create abstract colour schemes for each scene. We would keep deciding which range of colours – warm, cold, dark, pale, reds, blues – we would use for a particular scene: this would cover costumes, interiors and colours which would all come together. For the costumes we would choose fabrics, then scan them and print them off (the resulting photographs were quite lovely) in order to see how it would all look on film. Reasons would be given for choosing each of the colours used on screen and they would all be discussed. For example, I might say: "I really like how that blue blouse would look on Elena in scene so-and-so. Where might we use it again? Which scene would it be right for?" The whole world of the future film is thought through with reference to how colours and textures come together: we consider the way scenes echo each other, the powerful rhythms used for emphasis. Although the 'costumes-and-interiors' stage is not my province, I am involved nevertheless. That's because all the preliminary *artistic* work is necessary to ensure that the camera should *want to see* the story which Andrey wants to tell.

One of the main devices for motivating the camera is that together we should plan the space in such a way that the camera might hold the scene. After all, everything is based on the sequence of the actors' movements on the mise-en-scène duly prepared. It is not as if Andrey knows in advance precisely how a particular actor will move from one space into another space and how the two might come together. He may have guessed or subconsciously sensed it, yet quite simply the spaces in which we spend a good deal of time, are filming for a long time, they have been set up in advance in such a way as to determine certain rules of the game. If we take Sergei's flat, for instance... We deliberately asked Pankratov to prepare a flat that would be exactly like the mass-scale accommodation built in the Krushchev era – measuring 37-40 square metres. *That way* we pushed ourselves into a specific framework. We even decided not to use a removable wall when we were filming. When it came to Vladimir's space on the other hand it was the opposite situation: everything was arranged so that from any point in the flat it was possible to see even its most distant vista and that from any space (corridor, bedroom or study) it was possible within seconds to be in the kitchen. The space for the mise-en-scène was specially organised so that the actor could do a 360-degree turn. Moreover for the last scene an additional layer was added – the balcony onto which Sergei would go out with his bottle of beer and walk all round the mise-en-scène containing the women sitting by the television and then pat his son's head. Once again, without a pause, we go out with him into the open air, back to the trees and the crows and then re-immerse ourselves into the flat for the final scene. In that way nothing in Vladimir's flat interrupts the flow of movement. In Sergei's space though, movement is constantly being interrupted. Those two spaces are poles apart and the camera behaves in a fundamentally different way in each.

2. In Sergei's Home

So to Sergei's flat. The space is so crowded that the camera is physically *unable* to move. We had no choice – we could only stand there. Whichever way you tried to turn the camera, you would be up against a wall. There would always be an obstacle just standing there, getting in our way. Either a cupboard or a sideboard or some half-transparent door. You would always be seeing the scene *through something* – round a doorpost, the corner of a door or a sideboard. You would be working through a large number of surfaces with no texture to them, when a third of every shot would contain *nothing*. That would make everything feel cramped and uncomfortable – features of Sergei's world – but at the same time it would heighten the interest in that world. You felt you were looking out for something ghastly, peeping into it, spying on it. A very ordinary human pursuit, incidentally.

Moreover, as a result of the cramped space as a *principle of the filming*, in Sergei's flat the camera is unable to follow any character out of one room into another. The camera only does this once when it follows Elena out of the corridor into the sitting room (on that occasion, though, Elena enters like a guest from another world). Usually the camera just stands and observes, or presses up against the wall, when a character moves past, reduced in its turn to a mere object 'getting in the way'.

In the tight space of Sergei's flat we cannot just move smoothly on from one scene to another – only by a cut. This particular feature of the interaction between camera and space achieves an unusual visual effect: for instance when Tatiana goes out of the kitchen into another room where her husband and son are. Purely physical limitations make it impossible to follow her. This means that to move to where she is heading all we can do is switch everything off and then on again in a different place. Yet how can that be done while at the same time retaining a sense of movement? There is only one solution. Tatiana simply moves out of the frame, while we remain in the kitchen – in the frame which no longer contains her. After that we simply set up the camera in the room she was heading for, Sergei's bedroom, where he is sitting with his son – that is when she simply *comes in* to join us. In this way the camera is continually slowing things down. In the first instance letting a character move on while it lags behind and, in the second, waiting for the character to appear. This lingering camera lends a special syncopated rhythm to the whole space of Sergei's flat: movement then a pause, a jerk and then a pause. All the characters in it are engaging with each other and then trying to break away from each other. Relations between them are brittle, incoherent, chaotic and at the same time too close for comfort. In art, space is what characterises those who inhabit it: it is part of their portrait, a manifestation of their means of survival.

Once more I should like to make the point. *Technically speaking* it is always possible somehow to adapt space for our convenience. We even went through the technical process of making a removable wall in Sergei's flat, so that we could use 'travelling' shots. In Soviet films that was a technique often used. It was then easy for the camera to show characters moving to and fro and show the flow of one scene into the next. The camera would do that because it was not prepared to accept the *limitations* which reality placed on both camera and viewer. It was determined not to see what was actually going on in those spaces. This meant the Soviet camera remained blind to those limitations and simply knocked down the barriers of the world which it was itself creating, breaking out of its tension. It robbed us of those shots which would have conveyed the truth of that world.

In one of the interviews he gave I remember hearing the producer Alexander Rodnyansky say that he was struck – as a viewer – by what he saw through a doorway, when Sergei's wife Tatiana climbed up on to a stool to look for a bottle (so as to celebrate the arrival of the money). He caught sight of her plump bare legs cut across by her housecoat and that was all. For him, that image was extremely convincing, like an injection of truth.

I can remember that scene clearly, by the way. According to the original plan, when Tatiana suggests "celebrating/having a drink" and Sergei asks: "Why – have we got something?" and she answers: "Yes, we have", she was meant to leave the sitting room, go and get hold of a bottle and then bring it back in with her. Then, during the filming, we suddenly realised that it would all take place differently. She would go out and then with the help of a cut we would see her in the kitchen, where she would have to stand up, climb on to a stool, stretch and look for something 'higher up', while we would observe all that without moving, our backs pressed against the wall. If Tatiana left the room and then just come back with the bottle into the original shot... it wouldn't be *the same* scene. Why that was the case, why an 'exit' from the sitting-room would somehow secretly work against the spatial rules chez Sergei is something that could be analysed separately. Naturally – and I shall repeat it once more – you must always be careful not to foist on the camera *more* than you can actually see. The more of such limitations there are, the more precisely delineated the principles of imagery will be: after all art is, in essence, a strict selection of means to an end, an ascetic use of those means. Indeed that is why, when it comes to optics, I like to use only a small selection of lenses. That brings discipline into my interaction with spaces, with their rhythms. It lends a certain severity to the structure of a mise-en-scène.

If we compare the space in Sergei's flat with that in Vladimir's, the rhythm of movement in the latter is reminiscent of classical music or a ballet based on long sequences of uninterrupted movement of a body in an almost inanimate space. It is classical mechanics, the coldly calculated movement of stars and planets. The space in Sergei's flat on the other hand... is the opposite of classical. The movement there recalls in a certain respect the movement of the dancers in Matisse's painting 'The Dance' which also copes with lack of space, flatness and an absence of perspective and in which all those taking part resemble each other and are statically frozen in their poses, while their movement consists only in the transition from one 'spasm' to another. It calls to mind the decoration or pattern on a carpet, where movement is constant and at the same time completely static.

Here Matisse provides a good parallel. As in *The Dance*, so here the characters are presented 'decoratively', they are part of the interior. They blend in with the background, all the more so since they are 'incomplete' all the time, presented 'piecemeal'. Each character has his own piece of the patchwork, his own static little scene or pattern (the grandmother by the stove, the grandson at the foot of his parents' bed in front of the screen, the mother next to the disposable nappies and the father by the fridge) and these are all brought together to form a general recurrent pattern. This does not just apply to people. In this respect people are no different to things: there is the kettle at the same level as the hand which picks it up and with the shelf in the background. Yet at the same time (just as in Matisse's painting) we are nevertheless called upon all the time to detach the characters from that background, almost to cut them out: otherwise everything will freeze over once and for all and there will be no movement at all. I remember we had once been planning to use a corner-seat in that kitchen – a typical acquisition for families of that kind – but that uninteresting, one-dimensional fixture would have killed them all off once and for all, they would have drowned in their background. That was when Pankratov hit on the idea of the stools they sat on for meals forming the corners of a triangle. The family members are not comfortable – there are edges, lines, certain gaps in relation to the background, the sharpness of their triangular composition. Then the silhouette starts coming into its own – the outline, the back muscles, the arms... static 'movement' begins passing in a wave of nervous energy across the motionless fragments. This movement, this chaotic dance only serves to accentuate the background behind the figures, the aggressive nature of the setting, constantly seeking to swallow them up again, to make them 'revert'.

Another painter who grappled with similar tasks, was, of course, Edvard Munch. The lines defining his space were not lines of straightforward perspective; they were constantly touching and distorting each other, giving the beholder's gaze no room to expand. Munch positions perspective behind the figure, immediately before the beholder, looking out from the frame, straight at him. For the normal eye this is an alarm signal. To be honest, however, it has to be said that I was only really carried away by Munch *after* working on *Elena*, because it was only then that I was able properly to appreciate what he is actually doing, how he creates the sense of abandoned doom, his schizophrenic dance of chaos... If we did indeed arrive at Munch of our own accord, in the course of our work, so to speak, certain references to art had already been introduced. To Van Gogh's *The Potato Eaters*, for the scene in the kitchen, when they are all sitting round the table and the only warm light falls from the lamp onto Elena with the baby. There are several deliberate references of that kind from the history of art and probably they, in their turn, give rise to other associations of which we were not yet aware and which were not deliberate insertions on our part. At any rate our 'spaces' are not quotations from other canvases, but rather aesthetic endeavours, which may coincide with those confronted on numerous occasions in the history of visual art. If images from *Elena* appear convincing, it is not because they 'resemble' real life, but precisely because they have passed through a process of 'aestheticisation'.

This aestheticisation is extremely important. You may talk about lack of form, but you cannot do it lacking form yourself. One might talk about lack of meaning, but at the same time you are obliged to do so coherently. Lack of shape, lack of character, lack of rhythm or a statement ruin the shot. If you do not lend it anything aesthetic, then the best you can hope for is glorified television. In our film it is the characters who watch television, the viewers are experiencing *cinema*.

3. In Vladimir's Home

Of course we would hope that the two spaces – belonging to Vladimir and Sergei – speak for themselves but, in actual fact, the second space 'gains' from the first. It is precisely the *contrast with the first* that produces the *exaggerated* horror of the second. If we had not shown Vladimir's world right from the beginning, Sergei's space would not have looked *like that*, the level of despair would not have been the same. It is as if we find ourselves in a swamp after a clean and roomy space.

Within Vladimir's space we had sought to convey a sense of his smooth strength. Here it is easy for the camera to accompany an actor and it can do that for a long time. There is always plenty of light and air around a figure and for the camera it is of interest to follow how a character moves and behaves. In Vladimir and Elena's flat it is even possible to turn away from an actor and watch a crow outside the window, if that is the direction in which the beam of the beholder's gaze is turning. Here, space and freedom for the camera to enjoy a free life of its own is completely justified. At the same time we had sought from the outset to fill the shots with the smooth flow of a measured, thoughtfully planned life – the very kind which Vladimir had built up for himself. A flow like that is conveyed most effectively of all through the movement of the actors. Vladimir and Elena function together as an ideal unit, both participating in a shared rhythm, like that of two ballet dancers. This is how we film them in the constant spin of a 'figure-of-eight': she starts a movement and he takes it up or sometimes the other way round. Her space, then his space. He got up and left the flat, she got up, did something and went out into the kitchen: he came back from the bathroom and she made the bed. All that was one shot. No full-stops, no cuts. In addition, there is nothing else to do in that space but watch the movement of bodies: there are only general views and middle-ground shots, no close-ups. All the figures are visible in full.

Yes, it is an interesting meditation creating complex visual concepts of luxury and poverty. In Sergei's home the poverty is conveyed through the cramped space, the jerky rhythms à la Munch-Matisse, while in Vladimir's space it is possible to note certain astonishing echoes of other 'principles' from the history of art. It is precisely through the glow of light on certain objects that Zurbaran and Caravaggio depict luxury. If there is light, the beholder can also step back, can contemplate... Luxury is spaciousness, cleanliness. Luxury in life is when everything can be embraced in a single shot.

To include all this in a single shot also involves mathematical precision of course and it is not easy to calculate the movements of the camera in advance. We are following Vladimir into the bathroom, for instance, and we cannot go any further after that, so there has to be a pause. Then Andrey and I start calculating the camera movement differently: we both realise that it is important not to break off, so that the river should go on flowing, so that we should come onto the set the next morning and *exist* together with the characters. That smooth, uninterrupted flow of time and life is shown for a long time – for a period of one and a half or two minutes. Then editing takes over and we cut to breakfast.

Of course working within Vladimir's space was more interesting for me. There was call for more inventiveness. It was like an aquarium, in which what I was really keen to do was work with light.

For example, if you remember the scene when Vladimir had just lain down to write his will and Elena left the room, did some washing-up, went into the library and took down a medical reference book. Here, as was the usual routine, a single shot was used for all that. At the moment when she is in the kitchen, the sun is shining into it and the light-mood is a positive one. Yet, as we move with Elena into the library and she takes down the book – the lights fade, grow dimmer. We see that there is *no* sunshine in the library. When all is said and done, the desired effect is achieved: when Elena leaves the kitchen, the sun is shining on to the back of her neck and she is wrapped in a golden aura, but when she goes back there to carry out what will follow, it is with a totally grey face. After the appearance of that 'grey face', there then follows the episode with the burning of the papers. We wanted to film all of that with a single shot as well. So we kept on following Elena. First of all Elena is sitting down and looking at the photographs of the family displayed on the wall. Our gaze focuses with hers on a photograph, on a dark forest path, where she is still a young woman, happy and full of energy. After that Elena makes her first difficult attempt to rise to her feet. She stands up and at that moment we 'grasp' hold of her and capture her in a single shot. By this time though the camera is entirely steered by Elena's movement. First she stands up to her full height and then we see her, from her knees up. When she suddenly sighs and falls on to the floor, we again take in all of Elena – arms, legs, head, her whole body. We see Vladimir's body lying there and we see how Elena starts to hurry to and fro, to tidy everything up. After that she runs into the kitchen, takes out a dish and throws all the papers into it. Then our gaze is gradually drawn closer to her face. Yet this occurs through the flames. The glow from the burning paper starts from the bottom and lends Elena a slightly demonic air, as if her face is masked. Perhaps this is a cliché, but it conveys the right message. By this time we see before us not a grey face but one from Hell. We are never going to see the original Elena again, we are confronted now by a different person. Yet it is only Vladimir's space that makes it possible to convey the whole 'course' of the mutation of her *face*. Inside Sergei's space it would have been impossible to demonstrate such movement in the inner life of a single character.

In general, from the *cinematographic* point of view only three of the characters have a face – Elena, Katerina and Vladimir. That is because they all belong to the same 'metaphysical' space and Elena – unlike her children – does as well.

Yes, for no sooner has she entered Sergei's flat, than a semblance of order is established in it, for a moment at least. Even her coat which she hangs tidily on a hook, immediately starts to look like a Greek column standing out from the surrounding ruins.

That's an interesting observation. As for Elena (Nadezhda Markina) there's an amazing ambiguity about her appearance, which was what caught Andrey's attention. Facing forwards, Elena looks like just another ordinary woman, but her profile is undeniably Grecian. When she puts up her hair, then she has a truly Grecian air about her, she could be the wife of a king. It is interesting, beyond question, to exploit that, to create visual signs for the shifts in meaning we need. Elena's very nature is fluid, it changes and fluctuates. Given that objects in Vladimir's space (glass, wood, fabric) acquire an expressive texture of their own, it is quite feasible when creating Elena's portrait to concentrate, for example, on just her hair and this too has an impact. Each time her 'hair' seems to have a different texture, to reflect a different mood.

Sometimes it is Renoir hair and sometimes Velasquez hair... I assume that depends on the message being put across.

Definitely. Incidentally, the mirror, in front of which Elena is sitting, also has a story to tell. It's a dressing-table mirror. I don't know where it sprang from. It was probably Andrey Ponkratov's idea, when he was assembling props. At first glance, you think: what could be more banal than that? A dressing-table mirror in a woman's bedroom, where she can naturally be seen from three different angles. Yet at a certain moment the effect is very powerful – precisely after the crime, when Elena is sitting and looking at herself, but in actual fact not at herself, but at 'both women' in the side mirrors, at two reflections of herself. The contrast with the beginning of the film is a stark one: when she was sitting in front of the dressing-table in front of the mirrors, she had been looking not at her doubles, but at the light coming through the window. It may seem strange, but originally we had not had that effect in mind. We only grasped it when we were on set. Quite simply, when Markina sits down in front of the dressing-table and you begin to move the side panels, bringing them in closer, then you suddenly become aware of *this*. You see how it works and to what end. If someone else had sat down there and the same effect had not materialised, then there would not have been any play of reflections. If another actress had been playing the part, we would have closed the mirrors instead, just opened them a crack or even removed the panels – just one mirror would have remained and we would have ended up without four Elenas at once. We would just have had the hair bun, which she pins in place and that would have been all. Just the back of a neck.

As for Vladimir (Smirnov) his face was much more clearly defined than in Elena's case. In general he had an air of Julius Caesar, even his hair-style was appropriate: all that is missing is the laurel wreath. He has no 'second' face, he has been sculpted into just one. The similarity between the two main characters and the difference between them are used to convey many additional effects, particularly during dialogues, when one moment they are equals and the next far from it.

In the scene in Vladimir's kitchen the camera functions purely along gender lines. The camera also goes along with the male domination. One could say that this gender principle in filming is already ancient history, that it is almost always better to film a woman from above, when the axis of the camera is slightly above the eye-line. At the level of the forehead is better for filming the face. In this case, though, I am not filming a model or stereotype, but the very essence of the action. This type of shot can demonstrate how a hero dominates a heroine. Indeed when it comes to Katerina I'm filming the actress from below! Firstly because I'm filming her from the point of view of her father Vladimir, lying on the bed, and secondly I am making her appear slightly taller than she really is: here a woman, a daughter, is dominant.

Elena is a traditional woman, while Katerina is a rebel. Elena is repressed, Katerina is free. Elena hides her feelings, Katerina is open about hers. It is interesting to note that in classical European painting the image of a woman reflected in a mirror is precisely that of a poisoner. Artistic tradition and the camera's 'tricks' coincide here as well. Here too 'the woman in the mirror', Elena, is the principal and most powerful figure from the beginning of the film to its culmination.

Yes, and when she cries in the dark in Sergei's flat, she is looking almost straight at the camera, once again as if into a 'darkened mirror', straight at the viewer.

That, as I see it, is not a coincidence and not a quote: simply the introduction of those principles according to which European visual arts function and from which they derive their meaning, principles which various artists from various eras have embodied using a variety of materials. If we also add that a woman sitting motionless in front of a mirror is an image frequently found in epitaphs, then Elena can be seen to have been presented right from the outset as some kind of classical grave-side statue...That makes of the whole film some kind of lament, a lament for something that is dead and gone...

'Visual signs' create a special language of their own, their own texture of images above the level of content. These images possess their own degree of freedom and they are lifted above the content, heightening the impact of the story being told. It is precisely this which we might refer to as 'visualisation'.

4. Visualisation

I remember how in the nineties a friend took me into an editing suite and said: "Take a look." There was nothing out of the ordinary. A reel was fixed in place and a remote clicked into action. I came to understand how to mark a cut-off point, how an image taken from two angles, from two starting-points, can then be shifted to a third and how it is possible to mix images. I have always liked buttons. Here it is interesting that with the help of buttons you can immerse yourself in a shot, cut it, combine it with something else, turn it into something black, change its colour and even write some kind of nonsense over it. Introduce something of yourself into it.

I remember the first thing I ever edited. I just took a reel – some tourist views of Australia – and added a music-track from some song or other. In that tourism reel everything had been filmed very well, using short vivid shots. I put together a three-minute clip from that 15-minute film. I sweated away over it for two weeks. It was interesting how a series of visual images, which had nothing to do with the content of the song, could suddenly seem to match and be appropriate, provided the right rhythm was found. This utterly formal approach to the task turned out to be truly fascinating. By this time there were Australian planes flying in the song, rugby players running along the beach and hotels greeting their guests: the way all this was meshed with the rhythms and tunes created new editing sequences. That was my first attempt at 'visualisation'. The point is that films are there not just to inform and reflect. They are able, via a host of different images, even images that do not seem connected with the main content, to reveal and intensify the *meaning* of whatever subject is being treated. Enabling the beholder to *see* the meaning of something does not mean just illustrating and copying a subject.

Let us take, for instance, the conversation between Vladimir and Katerina in the hospital. The episode is filmed in such a way that we do not understand who is standing by the window. That was done deliberately. Vladimir is shown in clear focus, his profile is impressive and strong: then behind him there is a kind of white space and someone is standing *there*. Technically speaking, we wanted to have a background that was as blurred as possible, to blur the splendid trees outside the window behind Katerina. We were very worried that they might come into flower. So we had to shoot the hospital scene early enough to make sure there was no blossom, although buds had already appeared on those trees. We went all out to ensure that we would be dealing in blacks, whites and greys. There was no room for shoots or new greenery, because *she*, Katerina, does not want children. Green leaves would have clashed with the black-and-white colour scheme assigned to Katerina. All that was required was light. Otherwise just a charcoal drawing, static, austere, lit from above...

That is probably why the most important thing we see at the beginning of the episode is not even Vladimir's profile, but his ear, large and scrawny, a coiled shell. Then come the opening words: "I can hardly see you". So this makes an 'ear' a perfectly appropriate image for his 'hardly seeing'. If he can 'hardly see' her that implies Vladimir is 'hearing' her: the lean shell of his ear is taking in sound.

An interesting thought, although on a more everyday level what Vladimir means is – "You don't come and see me, you're a rare visitor". His daughter responds by saying: "it's because I'm standing against the light." She does not give a direct answer, but 'changes' the subject. She means that "the light is behind my shoulders" which could be taken as meaning "I'm letting in light here...". So it makes it quite natural for Katerina to have been positioned with her back to the window. As it streams through the window, the light almost appears to absorb the girl. Yet as soon as she says *something*, words 'reach' the ear and the focus immediately shifts to where she is standing and we realise it is the daughter. Moreover, she is dressed in something bluish-green, like a delicate reed, a living plant or a wave of liquid (she steps towards Vladimir, drinking water and thus bringing him life).

In essence, if we are able to step back from the concrete objects and figures in the scene, what we are actually seeing is a landscape. A man-mountain is spread before us, a pile of stone, with a profile for its ridge. In front of it or him there is a small tree, a reed, which later on sways in the wind and announces that it is standing against the light, is in the light and happily indulges in word-play, something familiar since childhood. Indeed the tree is joking with the mountain by the end of the episode. By that time only someone blind or deaf would fail to question whether the tree is the "daughter of a hedonist" – as Vladimir maintains, or in fact a being capable of affection.

There is a certain degree of visual dialogue between the mountain and the tree, between the inanimate and the animate, but at the extreme edge in this void – in this "I can hardly see you", "Answer me" – we have a dialogue of Man with God, for whom ever since the 19th century 'landscape' has been the purest mode of expression... It calls to mind Lermontov's words in our children's anthologies: "By a cliff a golden cloud once lingered on its breast...".

Yes, that is the simple poetry of our childhood. Yet it is worth stressing once more that this poetic dimension is created by an actual camera – encumbered this time not by the constraints of living-space (the space of this particular hospital was selected, incidentally, as matching most closely of all the rhythm of Vladimir's flat – spacious, light and convenient) but by the constraints of the relationship between two of the characters. If we return now to my Australian example referred to at the outset, in *Elena* we have the reverse situation. We do not deviate from the text but keep to it as closely as possible: we oblige ourselves to convey its content (characters and dialogue), but after that we need to create an energy field of a kind in which everything will be transformed into a new substance. If we talk of what our 'visualisation' is aimed at, it is precisely towards the creation of an extraordinary depiction of seemingly ordinary events. After all what is required of cinema is that it should intensify content, interpret it, maximise its possibilities – to the level of a religion... where the very profoundest questions can be touched upon.

If we take the scene of the fight, for instance. That is the 'space' inhabited by Elena's grandson, Sasha, and it is quite separate from that of Sergei or Vladimir. It is filmed differently as well – with a hand-held camera. Initially I was moved with the camera, but then I took over, I was doing the moving. It was a new way of filming, but I insisted that the scene be shot with a hand-held camera. Yes, the scene comes over as torn out of context, shot differently from the rest, but I could *see* that something quite different was taking place. There was nothing for it – the scene really was different from all the rest.

The camera is hand-held, it bounces up and down, it gets in the way. Later on, Andrey even asked the visual effects team to stabilise the image. Now though, it would be interesting for me to take another look at it and see whether that really had been necessary or not.

If we give some thought to the question as to why the fight is different, then you might say that Sasha is the 'third generation' in the story, another level of life's 'savagery' confronting us with a truly 'wild' man. There were woods or trees in this film ever since the beginning. It is the same jungle encroaching on life, the same bare trunks and branches which have, from the outset, been threatening the 'civilised world': they had stood outside the window of Vladimir's hospital bedroom, crows perched on them had been looking into the windows of his home. The forest is of the gloomy variety and now it is full of movement. The fight does not even seem to be of a human kind...the trees seem to be fighting amongst themselves... At night, in black darkness, in a tangle of dense branches. The desolate wind roams through the trees, as if it were foretelling something terrible, the very end of the world. Through an abandoned Garden of Eden... it had after all been an apple orchard. When we first went there and realised that was where we would do the filming, apples were crunching underfoot.

5. Shots

A shot is a combination of indivisible component parts. As soon as we start trying to divide it up into individual 'building blocks', everything collapses and the shot will soon be 'dead'. Everything loses its impact straightaway. It's like a virtuoso and his cello. He is the music which he plays. He is that music, he even moves like the music and I cannot say which comes first – music or musician. This human-cello is an extreme image of music, the last limit in music which can be 'depicted'. It is this image which quivers at the very edge of music. We have to film using visual entities which might constitute a maximised external representation of *invisible semantic energy*.

In each shot the important question is whether it belongs to the film or not. Sometimes I get carried away by some minor detail, side-tracked by an actor's movement or by flickering light and I might lose touch with the whole. Becoming side-tracked like that can lead to us starting to shoot a slightly different film from the one we had had in mind. Andrey may well put a stop to this and move us back to the point at which we had moved off at a tangent so as to continue in a different direction. It is Andrey who steers the film as a whole.

For me the shot is everything. It is a source of real happiness when light, colour and texture all come together, when quite apart from any technical diagram all the parts fuse and feed off each other so completely that eventually I see my very own self in my camera eyepiece – I see myself in *there*. It is not a portrait of me, but rather the current of my energy, which is more than just me. And all of this taken together – is simultaneously alive and lifeless, a fabric of images accessible only to the cinematographer. When all is said and done, what it is that I am seeing... three-dimensional reality, still palpitating, still alive, but already wrested free from objects and beginning to turn into a two-dimensional image. This is the last time I shall see it in transition. Next time we meet it will already be on film and two-dimensional, ready to be projected on to a flat wall or screen. It will be part of the flow in the film as a whole.

When it comes down to it, your personal pleasure is a migrating-image not fixed in reality or in film – something that is subtly distinct from both 'reality' and 'film'. It has its own right to exist, its own fleeting life. It is the potential for transition, for mutation, for alchemy.

"A gentle move to the inevitable, away from countless fears,
Away from weeping relatives and my own funeral's tears..."

What is that?

It's Baratashvili[44], as translated by Pasternak[45]:
 "Colour...that heavenly blue –
 As I boy, I loved that hue..."
 Sometimes lines of poetry surface in my mind of their own accord. I am no expert, unfortunately, but some verses I really do love. When

---

[44] Nikoloz Baratashvili (1817-1844) – a Georgian poet.

[45] Boris Pasternak (1890-1960) – a Russian poet, novelist and literary translator.

I was with Andrey in New York I discovered first Brodsky[46] and later Mandelstam[47]. That particular poem I came across completely by chance. I understand what it's about. It tells of the wonderful gradation of blue, has a deep understanding of blue, it speaks of things most complex *via* the colour blue... If it were possible to *film* that kind of blue, an amazing film could be achieved.

In general if you once sense that something has come out right, that you really have a shot, an image, that at the same time something is happening to your whole being, then you begin to realise that your life has grown five minutes longer. That's what makes doing all this worthwhile. Art is, after all, always concerned with the immortal... Why bother otherwise? It would not be worth our time and energy.

---

[46] Joseph Brodsky (1940-1996) – a Russian poet and essayist.

[47] Osip Mandelstam (1891-1938) – a Russian poet and essayist.

THREE INTERVIEWS. QUESTIONS TO THE DIRECTOR

ON THE APOCALYPSE AND NEW PATHS TO HOPE[48]

Yulia Balakshina: Our brotherhood has recently been thinking quite deeply about what is happening to humankind. In one of the Psalms it is written: "What is man, that thou art mindful of him?" – a being seen by God and made in His Image. At the same time, what we see around us very often puts us on our guard and frightens us. It was against a background of these considerations that we watched your film. It was like an unexpected message, which really resonated with what we had been thinking about. What can we do to make sure that man's inner world does not slam shut, so that God still has someone to remember and that there should be something in man for him to be mindful of? We imagined that this meeting would take the form of a conversation – like a dialogue, not a press-conference.

* * *

Andrey Zvyagintsev: I remember an impression I had when I was thirty. It was during the 1990s. I saw a documentary film called *The Vanishing Object* about a certain Obolensky, an actor who might even have been starring in an Eisenstein film, in early silent films at a time when the cinema was only just taking shape. In one of the fragments of the film he says that when he had been acting for almost fifty years

---

[48] On March 18, 2012 a group called 'Church Social Initiatives' of the Preobrazhensky Brotherhood organised a meeting in the assembly hall of the Saint Filaret Russian Orthodox Christian Institute. Members of the Preobrazhensky Brotherhood, students and teachers of the Saint Filaret Institute and parishioners from various Russian Orthodox churches in Moscow discussed Andrey Zvyagintsev's latest film *Elena* with him. The discussion was chaired by Yulia Balakshina and Alexandra Kolymagina, editor-in-chief of the newspaper *Kifa*. This is an abridged version of the discussion. For the full text see: *Kifa*, No. 6, May 2012 or the website www.az-film.com

(and we know how the Church regards actors, people who engage in dissembling) he suddenly found himself up against a brick wall, no longer understanding what he was doing. He relates how he then went to see his spiritual father and said: "I do not understand why I exist at all, why I have devoted fifty years of my life to this profession... What am I *doing*?" He had doubts as to whether he was on the right path and wondered whether he ought to change something in his life. The father confessor gave him the following answer: "Stay where you are. What you are practising – the actor's craft – is called upon to soften hearts, because the truth can only enter a soft heart." It was precisely that phrase which made such a strong impression on me and which I've never forgotten. It could be said that the phrase to some extent relieves people in the art world of responsibility, since in a certain sense it implies that art is an intermediary activity, even one providing a service. At any rate, so that I might be properly understood, I should like to stress the following: art is not itself truth, but it serves truth by 'softening hearts'. That is how I interpret the words which I heard back then.

Alexandra Kolymagina: I was surprised by a coincidence which occurred slightly outside the framework of your film – how it coincided with the subject and content of the last meeting of this kind to be held here, attended by Olga Sedakova, when we were discussing the Russian catastrophe of the 20th century and its consequences. People were saying that characteristic features of post-Soviet man are cynicism and fatalism, which find expression in, among other things, the belief that certain actions, which in principle should not be undertaken, can allegedly be contemplated in some circumstances: "for the sake of the Motherland", "for the sake of the family", and so on. This idea links in with your film in an uncanny kind of way. Yet during that previous meeting there was at least a glimmer of hope to be felt, hope that from out of the hopelessness of our general situation it might be possible to "strive towards resurrection" without which we would not be able to imagine any kind of future. I think there was far more hope in your previous films. In this one there is virtually none (though I might be wrong). Why is this? Both in *The Return* and *The Banishment* there is some light in the darkness, some expectation that the characters might change. Whereas here, the general feeling is far more that of a dead-end...

Andrey Zvyagintsev: So you are not even asking about what is there on the screen, but about what is happening to me personally? It is possible that I am filled with some kind of tragic awareness. It is difficult to fight against that, because that is a feeling with a mind of its own, outside my control, but one that can be observed and one which I cannot just choose to remove at will. If I were to create some different intonation at the end of the picture, I would be deceiving people, deceiving myself together with that awareness alive within me. If I do not believe in a different outcome to that story, why should I pretend, why should I create certain models offering a conventional ending: retribution, punishment, repentance? That was not just my idea - it was shared by both my co-script writer, Oleg Negin, and myself. The artistic director, for example, took a somewhat different view of the film. He had a rather different angle on *Elena*. A more complex one. He found it difficult to connect to her – not because there is no hope in the film, but for other reasons of his own. I think, however, that they were probably dictated by the very gloomy nature of thoughts about everything that is happening to us.

Yulia Balakshina: When Elena comes into the church and places a candle before the icon, she does not go over to the picture of Nicholas the Wonder-worker, to which the candle-seller had sent her, but to the icon depicting the 'Presentation of the Mother of God in the Temple', an image which is the very opposite of the idea of idol-worship. Was that a deliberate move?

Andrey Zvyagintsev: I shall perhaps be disappointing you or even astonish you, but it really was like that. We could not go into a functioning church (the Church of St. Zosima and Savvatii) and start re-hanging the icons. This was not a film set. To show what we needed, we had to follow Elena down a long narrow corridor and then she moves to the right and goes up to the icon. We had to be able to see her from the back, because the next shot was a portrait of Elena in close-up, when we see all sorts of 'infernal' images[49] behind her. You probably

---

[49] In accordance with tradition there are typically paintings on the subject of the Last Judgement on the west wall of a church (*Editor*).

noticed there was something most unusual there: 'God himself' sitting on a throne and, moreover, the fresco was unfinished. Perhaps not everyone saw what was behind Elena's back, but that was not what was really important to us. We even took the close-up at another place on the wall, so as to have a particular depiction as background – behind her left shoulder is a red devil holding an infant on his knees.

    So that's all there was to it: Elena walked up to the icon depicting 'The Presentation of the Mother of God in the Temple' simply because precisely that icon had been hanging there. I think it highly unlikely that anyone would have noticed that Elena walked up to one icon and then stood in front of another and so we were able, naturally, to film her reflection in the glass of the icon to which the candle-seller had directed her. For me the point of this episode was that Elena had heard to which icon she should go but then went up to the first icon she saw and that is where that episode then breaks off. As it seems to me, all the steps she takes after that are ones which are suggested to her. Simply, at that point, she had also decided to linger for a moment and perform a ritual. The key thing which is going to surprise you is the following. When we had decided that we would be filming in this particular church and in the way we eventually did (that was a few weeks before the filming) I asked what kind of icon that was. Father Alexander, who serves in the church of St. Zosima and St. Savvatii, told me about it. It is a very old icon (in fact there are many antique objects in that church) and when he told me about its subject, I thought to myself that we had come across a most striking coincidence. The actress Nadezhda Markina is a believer and I think even a regular church-goer. When we had already talked to her during the filming about that episode (precisely what she was to do and how – as a director normally would in discussion with an actress), I told her for some reason about the strong impression made on me by the surprising coincidence: there was one mother, a mother-to-be, and here was another. Before I had even finished telling her about my thought, she had collapsed onto a bench. She had grasped all the implications – regarding one and the other victim. So that is precisely how this particular coincidence 'works' for me.

Yulia Balakshina: For many of us that was like the 'starting point' in this film.

Andrey Zvyagintsev: You understand that most people do not, of course, realise what that motif is. In general, time and again you realise quite clearly that a particular element in the film people won't notice or pay attention to, but for you yourself it's important to include it. You feel good at the mere thought that a particular meaning is there in your film. I'm glad that you noticed it. Although, on the other hand, you are the very people who would have noticed it.

Yulia Zaitseva: I should like to take Alexandra's question one stage further. As far as I know the script was originally based on the subject of the apocalypse. Is that the case?

Andrey Zvyagintsev: Yes[50].

Yulia Zaitseva: Perhaps that is what you understand by an 'apocalypse'? Just a catastrophe or end?

Andrey Zvyagintsev: Without any hope? Is that what you mean?

Yulia Zaitseva: Yes. For you there is no glimmer of light in an apocalypse?

Yulia Balakshina: But the Apocalypse ends with the image of New Jerusalem[51].

---

[50] "When I talk about the apocalypse I mean the following. Elena is that very battle field, where inside a person a total collapse of moral principles takes place. She simply falls apart, without herself realising that. Inside her an apocalypse is taking place, the individual is being diminished right down to the very core or the last atoms of that person. I gave an interview about those ideas, in which the word 'apocalypse' was used quite frequently, because I had been living in the midst of that theme. It is precisely that which I would refer to as an 'apocalypse' and that is what is taking place within our territory, within individuals here in our country (May 29, 2011, Andrey Zvyagintsev on the television programme 'Pozner').

[51] "And I saw a new heaven and a new earth: for the first heaven and the first earth were passed away; and there was no more sea. And I John saw the holy city, new Jerusalem, coming down from God out of heaven, prepared as a bride adorned for her husband. And I heard a great voice out of heaven saying, Behold, the tabernacle of God is with men, and he will dwell with them, and they shall be his people, and God himself shall be with them, and be their God. And God shall wipe away all tears from their eyes; and there shall be no more death, neither sorrow, nor crying, neither shall there be any more pain: for the former things are passed away" *Revelation 21:1-4.*

Andrey Zvyagintsev: Yes, there is always light somewhere. We are still continuing to exist, to breathe, to live. We allow ourselves to make a film – the first one, and then venture to make the next one. *Elena* is just one view-point, one slice of reality, no more than that. It does not claim to make any colossal generalisation. I'm sure you'll agree that in the soul or heart of every human being there are moments when you realise that life is intolerably hard. That's where this film comes from. Then you just need to imagine a cardboard New Jerusalem which could have been put on the screen immediately after the final credits.

Tatiana Avilova: In the interview entitled *Mirrors* a remarkable idea was expressed, namely that Elena was not just one particular individual. She does indeed represent a state of mind which is to be found, possibly not throughout our society, but in part of it. You said that you were trying to follow a life as closely as possible with a camera and show it as it really is. For a camera to film like that, white has to be white for the author of a film and black black. The system of co-ordinates for that person is very important. In similar situations, Lars von Trier, for instance, simply romanticises evil and sin and sometimes even justifies them. Something which is simply out of the question. Your system of co-ordinates arranges everything in its proper place: black is black, evil is evil and everything is given its proper name. A picture that comes to mind in connection with this film is Kramskoi's *Christ in the Desert (1872)*, which many people nowadays criticise for the fact that it does not, allegedly, show the true Christ. Yet he writes that what he wanted to depict was the dramatic situation of a moral choice facing a man of his times, the unavoidable moment in the life of each one of us, when we have to decide "to turn right or left, to betray our Lord God for a rouble or not to give way to Evil in the slightest". *Elena* is also like the moral choice facing people today: should they live lives dictated by animal instincts or perform acts of a kind which shall always "take us one step higher" as defined by Olga Sedakova.

I ask myself: does your Elena have the possibility of not yielding to evil? Or is she placed in a purely animal state, when she thinks of her cub and thinks for some reason that he is threatened by danger (although it is possible that in fact no danger actually threatens him)

– and that's it: reason doesn't come into it any more, no other path seems possible. In this sense your picture is, of course, horrifying.

Andrey Zvyagintsev: Does Elena have any basis for such a possibility? What choice does she have? What needs to be said first of all is that any individual always has a basis for such a possibility – it goes by the name of free choice. Whatever the individual might use to justify his actions later on, they always start out from that absolute freedom of choice which they have had from the very beginning and free of charge. A person makes their own decisions. And only they themselves are responsible. I think that in reality the whole film is about that. Our Elena is simply thrown back on her instincts. As Gurdjieff said: an individual who has not arrived at self-awareness is like an automaton. Elena acts impulsively, spontaneously, to save herself. This is because her relatives, her continuation, are another part of herself. Everyone in this film is concerned with themselves. Vladimir is in that same situation as well. Although difficulties do arise with this question – the ones you mentioned. You feel that all the accents have been arranged in position in the film: it is clear who has done what. Evil is evil. You said that everything is given a clear name. Not everyone responds to it like that though. Many people have said: "I would not have acted like that", or they have asked: "Why did Vladimir behave like that? What's he thinking about?". I feel that this is precisely 'Elena's state' – blindness and a total failure to understand: she is disorientated within her own space. What could be done to overcome that, I do not know.

Tatiana Avilova: This question is very important for us too, you know. I should like to mention an experiment which was carried out in the Soviet period. Not a very humane one. They tried to make people in a deep state of hypnosis kill others and watched to see if people were capable of doing that or not. It turns out that there are people capable of doing it. But there are people who break down – they become hysterical – they are quite simply physically incapable of carrying the task out. In our system of co-ordinates we understand that the ability to commit murder is a sign of an individual being psychologically damaged. Then comes the question as to what the roots of that psychological damage were. In your story Vladimir and Elena seem to

165

have been born like that. Nowhere is there any reference to who their parents might have been or whether there was any kind of background story. We don't know how they were brought up or why they're like they are when we see them. We see their children in the film, who are obviously their descendants. But where did they themselves spring from? That question is important for us too.

About a year ago the Saint Petersburg director, Oleg Dmitriev, paid us a visit and read us the script of his play *Bewitched by Death*, based on the book *Second-hand Era. The Demise of Red Citizens* by Svetlana Alexievich. In his play Oleg (he is a man of your age) was examining a similar question. He was aware of this psychological damage in himself. Indeed, if people tried to make any of us commit a crime while under deep hypnosis, we do not know how we would react, how deeply rooted we are in goodness or how far we have been able to avoid psychological damage? What kind of roots do we have? Do they enable us to stand up to this evil or not? Oleg Dmitriev says that he can feel his psychological damage, even at a genetic level. In his play there are a grandfather, mother and son – a man of his own age. The grandfather is an executioner, the mother was born in a concentration camp and the son is carrying in himself traces of this 'double heritage' of slavery. He feels a sense of imminent doom within him, a sense of doom that comes into its own in Elena too. Vladimir does not come over as someone fully alive either. Did you think about what might lie behind the present state of people in today's Russia, of your Elena?

Andrey Zvyagintsev: It is easy to see things in terms of heredity: executioner grandfather, time-server or embezzler father – that's the kind of people we are nowadays. Yet what does that explain? How does that help us? We could also say "our environment has poisoned us", "it's the fault of our genes". And so what? All we're doing is establishing a fact and that in itself does not give us any pointers to what we might do about the way we *ourselves* have turned out. As far as inhuman experiments are concerned, I don't think that's the right way to approach the question, since when under hypnosis a person is robbed of his own will. How can we form an opinion of a person or judge him, if he has no will of his own, when an experiment like that is being carried out? The individual determines his own independent choice, which has not been dictated by anyone or anything. Only in real conditions surrounding a choice and not in the simulated context of an 'experiment' is it possible for an individual to see himself or anybody else. Merab Mamardashvili[52] says that "the essence of being human lies in the effort to achieve that". What kind of human being are we talking about, if his very scope for trying to be human has been taken away from him by external circumstances? But now the background story of Vladimir and Elena and who their parents were.. We all have the same background story and parents: Adam and Eve and Cain and Abel. The idea you expressed – "it turns out there are people capable of killing" seems to me as innocent as it is naïve. Just look around you – there are plenty of people like that. Or ask yourself: who forced the first man to raise his hand against his brother? What kind of genealogy can you talk about then?

I shall now tell you – by way of an anecdote – a story about a British producer who, after reading the script of *Elena*, sent me a whole list of questions and comments (later we turned down the English-language project and parted company with that producer, but not because we failed to understand each other). He insisted that it was necessary to answer the numerous questions he had raised through alterations in the text of the script, not through correspondence. He suggested that it was necessary to clarify for the audience the background to all the events: to explain, for example, what the source of Vladimir's wealth was or why Sergei was out of work and so on. In other words, to do everything differently from the way it was in the film, in which the situation is a given and there are no hints or de-coding, simply a slice of reality: people taken unaware in their current circumstances. Without any commentary on their actions they function in the here and now. The producer wanted explanations for everything. And now comes the punch-line. He suggested (and this conversation was on the telephone): "Let's do a flashback? An episode from Elena's childhood. Let's show a scene of some trauma from Elena's childhood, which could explain why she committed murder." It was all I could do to refrain from commenting. Such banal Freudianism... What I want to say is that, if someone suggests a solution of that kind he thinks that all of his questions could be answered just like that, well then it's clear that he and I would definitely not be able to work together.

Tatiana Avilova: It's not really in relation to the film I'm asking but

---

[52] Merab Mamardashvili (1930-1990) – a Georgian philosopher.

for your personal opinion on that.

Andrey Zvyagintsev: I'm an idealist. In my opinion 'the cult of the Golden Calf' which burst upon us so suddenly out of the blue has simply shattered our society, which had been held together on some kind of basis at least. We had to throw ourselves into all those new unfamiliar activities and by then we had started to see any kind neighbour as no more than a rival. That was what happened to us all. And I feel all that will inevitably leave its mark. It's not a question of money, that's always been a cause of problems for people and a measure of what they're going through. The question is what kind of place it now occupies in our life in general now. It is money by which all values are judged: you can't get away from it. The principle of 'survival, at any cost' undermines all other values. Isn't that the catastrophe which will lead to changes in the human species as a whole?

Alexander Strotsev: Today an idea has been voiced in this auditorium to the effect that the key figures in this film are all of us. It has been voiced from very different standpoints: from the point of view of those who say "Those are people like us, we would have acted in the same way" and from your standpoint, when you use these words "people like us" with quite different implications. For me in this film it is very clear that you are not separating yourself from these characters and from what is happening to them and there is some hope, about which we have also been talking, to be gleaned precisely from that. But my question is – where do we find the strength to acknowledge that in ourselves? Very often you come across the fact that people, even those capable of telling it like it is and describing such problems, seem to turn their back on them and, as a result, they are not resolved.

Andrey Zvyagintsev (after quite a long pause): How else can we approach them? I simply don't know what other line we might take. You understand that you can only hold an audience's attention by telling the truth, by speaking directly about what you know, about what you see, even if that truth is stark and pitiless. You have to tell that truth and call a spade a spade. Another question and a very subtle one, which I am still grappling with myself, is what to do about people who are aware of this situation but simply shut their eyes to it. I don't know how to confront that. I don't know what kind of fabric has to be created so that people should *appreciate* that, should grasp that this involves *them*, precisely *them* – not in such a way that they should derive satisfaction from such a realisation, but as a wake-up call to make them think about themselves in a completely different light. I don't know. It's a question I'm still working on. What is, however, perfectly clear to me is that what we don't want to do is concoct fairy-tales – all those false saccharine renditions which lull us into a sweet sleep about ourselves. We need to talk about the real issue, what is important, what is really happening and what you actually see, what makes you worry about what is happening to you and society... Those may sound like highfaluting words, forgive me, but how else can you put it?

Aleksandra Strotseva: It's easy for someone to talk about what is happening to society and not to talk about what is happening precisely to him, precisely in the here and now. It's difficult to grasp that these processes are taking place inside him. I felt that you do recognise what's going on.

Andrey Zvyagintsev: I don't know all that's going on.

Tatiana Avilova: For me the most terrible thing was the last frame: the baby in the black space, not only on the bed of the departed – terrible in itself, but in general the radiant baby in the totally black space. Such a striking metaphor. Nerve-wracking. What was the thinking behind that image?

Andrey Zvyagintsev: Yes it is a frightening prospect. Many people have been saying that this image has this kind of impact. Everyone refers to that frame as the last, because that's how they remember it, although there is actually another one – the really last one. In that last frame people think they see crows, although there aren't actually any in it. There are only crows at the beginning. What does that image signify for me? Let me say that images are created so that each person seeing the film might form his own picture of what he has seen. The image is impossible to express definitively and perhaps, for that very reason, it has such a powerful impact. You must agree that it would be very banal, even vulgar, if I were to say, for instance, that the image of that infant symbolises the future. That shot, the angle used and the musical accompaniment, the whole mood which it presents to us is far more profound than narrow statements like that.

I should like to put to you what is perhaps an unexpected idea concerning Elena's choice of action. Very often people justify their actions by saying that they were all 'for the sake of the children'. In actual fact, I think (and this is just a suggestion, a guess, no more) that this is how people cover up the true reason for their fear of themselves. What she puts first is herself and not only the continuation of her line but her own welfare. However strange it may sound, those considerations are present. That's what that choice signified for me.

Olga Sinitsyna: I did not see your film today, I went to see it earlier with my mother. She is not a believer but I am a church-goer. She, of course, could not relate to Elena in that situation, but she nevertheless recognised herself – as I did. Because what the film actually portrays is a typical domestic family situation experienced by many of our post-Soviet families. Many things in the film come over as familiar. I watched the end of the film expecting retribution at any moment...

Andrey Zvyagintsev: There is emotional expectation... The film prompts us to think, to look for answers. I know that what is shown in the film is truthful but I don't know where to take it any further. Just imagine if those 'prescriptions' or 'directions' had came up on the screen instead of the final credits, which incidentally last five minutes – and that's a long time, long enough for a sizeable text, but what kind of answer would that have been? As I see it, that's precisely the tradition we're used to from Russian literature – questions being raised but not answered. Answers dispensed like that 'free of charge' have no value. Each of us needs to look for them himself. There are people who think the answer is clear: "I would have done the same". That's their responsibility, that's how they find their 'way-out'. What is there to say? That's the baggage they've brought with them to this point in their lives today and there's nothing to be done about it, unfortunately.

Igor Korpusov: It seems to me that there is punishment in this film. Let me try and explain what I mean. There is punishment in this film, because the life with which the film ends – endless watching of TV soaps, snacks and crisps, Elena's relatives who don't love her (you sense that when she visits them), that endless illusion of life, that grey routine which it is impossible to escape – that is perhaps more terrible than any actual punishment. Perhaps punishment would be a blessing seen from that angle. Hell (literally) is a place devoid of light. In their life there is no light, that's the hardest thing they have to bear.

I have had to guide visitors round sites connected with the grim history of Russia in the 20th century. The hardest thing is having to explain the reality of evil to people. They find it very difficult to believe that reality. When you tell them about certain terrible incidents, people shy away from it all, try to convince themselves that people couldn't behave like that – if they had been monsters then it would be conceivable. That leads them to think: "That problem doesn't affect me, because I'm not a monster". Yet, if those who did the torturing were human beings after all, then you have to relate all that to yourself. If the torturers were capable of such things, then it means I could be... Taking that on board is an almost impossible burden! Contemplating the possibility that I too could have shot those wretched victims... Imagining to themselves that evil is something banal is something which for some reason people find impossibly difficult. They imagine that evil has to be something special like the blockbuster *2012* or the end of the world – something myth-like, with everyone dying out.

Andrey Zvyagintsev: Like a show on Channel One Russia.

Igor Korpusov: Yes, something striking... but here we have a hell where everything is grey...

Andrey Zvyagintsev: The glass jar with the trapped spiders... Hell à la Svidrigailov... No light, but no darkness either, just greyness, murk which is even worse.

Irina Vasilieva: I have the impression that none of the characters has been able to tear themselves out of that pattern of life, out of the system in which they live: none of them has been able to overcome it. Even Katerina, although she's honest and truthful, even she is unable to admit that she needs to move on. An escape for her could be giving life to a child (there is a hint of that, in passing, in her conversation with her father). Yet for every character there is an escape route, if they make a choice. In Elena too something takes place, some inner resistance, but she was unable to stand up to the force which dictated her action to her at an instinctive level. Despite the depth of the gloom, into which any person can be plunged, all the same there is something that can help him climb out of those depths and come up on to the surface. You are clearly someone capable of brighter optimism, but where do you glean strength from and where do you see the opportunity for that resistance, so as not to make the choice portrayed on screen? Did you think that somewhere there are people, who would resist despite everything?

Andrey Zvyagintsev: There are people like that, of course, and there always will be. Yet it is absolutely impossible to go into all that in a 90-minute film plot. The screen cannot embrace them all, so what we have here is just one story and a small range of characters. That was how the film took shape and bringing more elements into it would not have seemed right or necessary.

As for me, personally – as I have already said today – I am an idealist. My education is nothing special: I have only chalked up two drama courses at university, one in Novosibirsk, where I was born, and the other in Moscow. I have to admit that training did not equip me with any basic, fundamental knowledge. The main focus in higher education in that field is always on acting skills and classes in those take up the lion's share of the time. Yet, during their studies, young people read great plays, great literature. Those works almost always portray brave heroes, who stand up to life's banality, the petty concerns of everyday life and refuse to betray their conscience. How should I put it...? Are you with me? When, after the age of sixteen, you have spent several years of your life immersed in texts by Shakespeare, Aeschylus, Racine, Chekhov, Dostoevsky and so on, I think you're bound to have had that injection of resilience you were talking about. I've never really asked myself that question, but perhaps that in itself is revealing. I don't mean to say that I always come out on top, no way... I don't regard myself as an adult even, for a long time I have been feeling like a child. At difficult moments, whatever choice has to be made, I measure myself up against one particular well-known character and understand straightaway what needs to be done. Everything becomes completely clear, but it is very difficult to take the next step, to find in oneself the courage to undertake the necessary action and follow it through. Perhaps that explanation sounds over-dramatic but that's really how it is. I don't have any other criterion, there's no-one to prompt me as to what I should do and how. I'm not even talking here about words, which might inspire me to act. No. What matters is the figure, the taciturn figure. Reference has already been made to the Legend of the Grand Inquisitor today. So that's it, His silence – Dostoevsky's invention of pure genius.

Anna Danilevich: First of all I should like to say thank you for your films. I watched your film on the one hand as a well-adjusted ordinary individual and, on the other, sometimes wearing my artist's hat and sometimes as a Christian. I was, of course, struck by how clearly you portrayed everything. When someone starts turning to God and begins to read the Holy Scriptures, he is bound to find out that there are two paths in life: the path of Life and the path of Death. They are very different from each other but the individual always has a choice – the freedom to choose the one or the other. I should like to thank you for portraying very clearly in your film how an individual does not necessarily have to make a special effort to set out on that path, he moves along it while just staying in his ordinary surroundings. If he does not attempt to rise up above himself, above his everyday routine, above his family and above his current circumstances, he is moving along the path of Death. As an artist, I kept watching how everything was being filmed and I was struck by the image of the baby, which has already been recalled by other people here. There is a whole iconography on the subject of the *Adoration of the Christ Child* and I remembered straightaway Botticelli's picture with its beautiful, brightly lit Christ Child. He is lying with his face uppermost. As you look at Him, you understand how everything is concentrated in Him, which would later be revealed in the course of history – all of Christian life and culture – everything through Him, all the Light which he brought into the world. Then we come to your shot, the penultimate one, where the baby is lying face downwards and one has a completely different response. It would seem that punishment has already taken place? At the same time, that small individual also has free will. But all those people have already planted in him part of the non-freedom to choose death. To what extent had you thought through all of that?

Andrey Zvyagintsev: I like that association very much. I'm grateful to you for it. I don't make out that we had thought about that in particular and invested it with that meaning. We almost didn't manage to wait long enough for the baby to go to sleep and whether he ended up on his back or his front – all that was accidental. The way scripts are written pre-supposes the possibility that – whether you intended it or not – certain additional meanings might manifest themselves. A film always turns into something more than you originally planned and you can say that about it, precisely because an image can unfold in the mind of the beholder and how it turns out will depend on whether it falls on fertile ground or not. If we *invent* something and decide quite simply to go out and film it, it will not work at such a 'deep' level. For example, the 'tone' about which you were talking, all the grey murk, the flow of banal ordinary life, which is a form of dying. After thinking about that, it is impossible to recreate it directly, because that would be an artificial decision and each shot would then be bereft of sunlight. The grey murk is not outside but inside. As for the frame with the infant, I think that your association evolved like that not thanks to way the shot had been filmed (the angle and the arrangement of the figure), but thanks to the whole flow of the film. The impact of the film is an accumulative effect involving a whole host of cultural and everyday associations and recognition of the tense meaning which the audience will sense at the end. A quite different issue is that for someone Botticelli's infant is just another child, an exhibit in a gilded frame hanging in a picture gallery. In order to glimpse the meanings you were talking about, you need to possess the *vision* which culture, education and reading true literature have imparted to you: then it's the luck of the draw – either you have the divine gift or the dough will never rise...

Oleg Glagolev: My question, to put it briefly, may well sound naïve. How are things now for Elena Anatolievna? What's happening? I wanted to ask whether you have the courage, whether there's any point in going further with that individual, to see how the person will live later on? Because there is hope that for as long as anyone is alive, the point of no return does not exist? Do you think it is necessary or possible to consider the development of that theme? I do not of course mean any 'Elena – Part II'. I am talking about a person who has stepped outside normal boundaries, who was prepared to step into darkness.

Andrey Zvyagintsev: I have said already that Elena does not exist. The film is over and there's no more Elena. She has just created an impression, as I said before, and planted some seeds of ideas in the audience which might make people think about themselves. That's what I see as the whole point. Let me repeat once more that the film and the characters in it are merely a possible trigger that can make people think about themselves.

MIRRORS[53]

Ksenia Golubovich: While preparing for this interview, I was struck by one thing which I encountered again and again, while listening to people's responses to your film. Everyone who talked about it and said how they interpreted it, started – essentially – 'denouncing themselves'. Identifying with one or other character, with one or other view of what this film had to say, they would point out which part of the 'Elena space' they inhabited. I read interpretations of the film from 'Elena's point of view', stating how those 'Vladimirs' – users and élitist snobs – got their just deserts. I read 'anti-Elena' pieces, in which she was presented as a terrible mother, "a monster with tear-filled eyes," (Limonov's[54] words) who castrates and paralyses her own children to such an extent that it would be for the best to remove her somehow from Russia altogether. I read interpretations 'in Vladimir's name' from the point of view of the élite which, if it wanted to say anything to the population at large, would comment: "You are all 'lay-about Sergeis', like Elena's sons, or 'barbarians', while we are the only people in this country who know how to work." I also read interpretations 'in Katerina's name'. It's obvious that there could also be interpretations 'in Sergei's name'. Basically, what we have are numerous interpretations of one and the same event, one and the same 'evil', which you could have shown in the film and which would have completely changed its meaning,

---

[53] Extracts from an interview: Ksenia Golubovich in conversation with Andrey Zvyagintsev. The full version of this conversation can be found at the site www.letterra.org. The interview took place in Moscow on January 28, 2012.

[54] Eduard Limonov – a Russian radical writer, stylist, organiser of the National Bolsheviks political party.

but at the same time... For me though, Elena is not the name of the central character, but that of a 'state of the world'. Lars von Trier called his planet 'Melancholia', meaning not just a rogue planet wreaking destruction but the actual state of the world facing that destruction. Melancholia. Loss of meaning. That is what you called 'Elena'.

Andrey Zvyagintsev: As for the audience, that happens practically all the time. When someone talks about a film, he is in actual fact talking about himself. A film worthy of the name is always a 'magic mirror' like that. I like the expression: "It's not only us watching films, but films watch us as well". It's just that in connection with *Elena* this is perhaps particularly noticeable. In this picture we can grasp and map out the logic of *any* character. Depending on whose logic is closest to us, that is how we will understand who is in the right. Whether Elena is a criminal for example. Someone told me that on their way out of the cinema they had heard two young women comment: "I would have acted the same way" and then "Me too". For them Elena's course of action was absolutely straightforward and logical. There was no question of any forks in the road or alternatives. For other people there is a 180-degree turn-around in how they view Elena herself and the other characters. I heard about that today: another film-goer was telling us how he had taken a negative view of Katerina, Vladimir's rebellious daughter, from the moment she had appeared on screen. He had thought of her as an impossible wretch, as a cynical rebel, but by the end he had come to realise that she was the real heroine. While, as regards Elena, everything was the opposite way round. At first he had sympathised with her: she had so many problems, she was taking care of her husband, while he did not take her into account in any way, as for her children, they did not take her into consideration at all. She was the sacrificial Mother. Then suddenly this mother – without batting an eyelid – starts killing, stealing and lying at every turn. The idea is simple: at first the viewers sympathise with Elena, feel sorry for her, look for their own traits in her, in other words 'a focal point of warmth, of love', through which they can absorb and understand what is taking place on screen, and then later they turn sharply away from her. More than that even, depending on their particular starting-point, Elena even ceases to be the main character in the film for some of them. That is because our viewing habits dictate that the main character should be the focus of our sympathy. If a break and a shift take place in the normal pattern, Elena becomes a secondary figure. She is stripped of the 'moral authority of a heroine and victim' and then Katerina assumes pride of place, despite the fact that she only appears in three scenes of the film. Yet, depending upon the viewers themselves, any of the characters can become the 'main' one. This is because, in the final analysis, we can watch the events from the point of view of any of the characters and the task of the material used in the film is to be able to withstand such changes, making sure that nothing is disrupted and that everything remains in place regardless of the interpretation. The film should at the same time remain complex and multi-layered, rather than flat. I would not want to make a film that is inward-looking, moving within the framework of a narrative in which pointers to the outcome are arranged in advance. For me it is intolerable to have a moralist on hand, who plays us the whole tune in advance, complete with intonation, and presses the pedal when required. The camera merely observes – that's the most important thing for us. Everything unfolds of its own accord, avoiding distortions. Each member of the audience comes up against himself, with whatever conflict he has been subconsciously carrying within.

KG: In that sense all the characters participate in and are part of this whole world. The characters are points of tension: for Elena to have taken shape, they all had to take shape. But if we talk about you as a viewer, where is your place in 'Elena's world' – how do you read it?

AZ: For me it's all very simple. I am very banal. For me murder is murder. That's all there is to it – full stop. What Elena actually does should not be done in any circumstances and that's why what happens is a personal disaster for her. Whatever kind of person Elena might be, I do not think she will be able to live with the consequences. It will be her undoing. From now till the end of her days she will carry that hell in her heart. There may not be any punishment in the film, but it will take place beyond the framework of the film, it will follow soon after the final credits. That's the human being speaking in me, not the film-director. In this respect, my choice of 'method' was key –

THREE INTERVIEWS. QUESTIONS TO THE DIRECTOR

precisely from the moral angle. I deliberately work against any logic of revenge and satisfaction through retribution in the confines of this film. People often compare *Elena* with *Crime and Punishment*, saying there's punishment in the novel but none in your film, forgetting that *repentance* precedes *punishment* in the novel. In responses I say: "Yes there is no retribution, definitely none before the credits and I think that's right because precisely that lack of retribution obliges you to think about it." When Elena's grandson goes off after the murder to a 'gang-battle' and is then seen lying on the ground after the fight, people in the audience think he's been killed and that will be her retribution – you want the action to come full circle. The energy stirred up by the film demands release. Now he'll die and it will all be over, the case will be 'closed' and you in the audience can at last draw a line under what has been a disturbing subject. Elena will no longer loom before you, forcing you over and over again to confront her in your inner cinema. The film is accomplished, the cycle has been completed. Here though, everything is quite the reverse. In that scene after the knife-fight, we filmed Sasha from a distance as he lay limp and lifeless on the ground. The camera's view of him is stretched back like a bowstring. We even used a computer to extend that scene for another twelve seconds. It had to remain unclear for a long time whether Sasha was alive or dead, whether punishment had been exacted or not. Then when Sasha suddenly comes to life, the audience gasps, but we don't let them breathe out again from that very moment right up until the final credits. There is a gasp, but no chance to breathe out again. It is perhaps cruel to treat the audience like that, but it was essential because we must not go on living the way we do, like witless chickens, in familiar deadening routines. Otherwise everything will be reduced to cotton wool – when you are told the same story for the thousandth time, a story which you already know by heart. An open ending or an open-ended pattern makes you go on thinking.

The same goes for the situation with the will. In this respect we took detailed advice from a lawyer. It turned out that if Elena had not married Vladimir, she would not have received anything. It could have turned out that the sacrifice would have been in vain. Yet, if she had been deprived of her inheritance – which would have involved just one line of the script – it would have had the same effect as 'killing off' Sasha, for whose sake she had committed the crime. That would have been retribution. But retribution was not what we were after. Everything remained in place as it were.

Yet I, myself – the person, not the film-maker – nurtured in a world of Russian culture, according to ethical principles from the old days – principles of the 'neatly rounded' form demanding retribution – naturally expect that beyond the final credits the horror of retribution is bound to catch up with her.

KG: It's strange but I saw the episode with Sasha simply as a continuation of the evil which Elena represents. After all, Sasha is the person for whose sake she committed the murder and *all he is,* is a youth on the margins of society, indulging in fights in the backyards and rubbish dumps of his world.

AZ: You know, before we started work on Elena, I experienced something I just couldn't shake off. I saw a man on TV of around fifty, more or less Elena's age. People off-screen were talking about him, recounting some news. I looked at his face, took him in, grew used to him and wondered who and what he was. Suddenly someone could be heard off-screen saying that he had killed his mother for the sake of 17 square metres of living space. It was impossible to imagine. As I looked at his face, I found it *impossible* to envisage that this fellow was capable of something like that. He was speaking calmly, nodding his head and it was clear that he was giving thoughtful answers to the questions he was being asked. What does 'art' usually do in circumstances like that? It lends such events an extreme emotional flavour. In real life things can work out very differently.

One of our major film-directors once said to me: "I can see that there is tremendous energy in you, a bomb of emotions just waiting to explode. Why are they all frozen stiff? Let go!" I have a different view of all this. The more ordinary Elena seems, the less she ponders, the more convincing she seems. Because that's the low-key way things play out. What's more that has a greater impact. If you have a scene full of nothing but emotion, that is just a one-off event. If, on the other hand, you have a scene like the one with that man on the television, where a murderer's face has nothing out of the ordinary about it, then you feel incredibly sad for mankind in general, for its future, for everything that's happening to us. It turns out that an unremarkable death, under our very noses, is something that does not let go of us. A man has killed and nothing reveals how that was possible. That is why Elena is as she is. People ask me why she "does not suffer". And at the same time they wonder why she weeps so bitterly at the funeral, such a hypocrite! I tell them that she is not a hypocrite: we had had trouble ensuring that she cried in a truly sincere fashion. She cried truly sincere tears. She had also cried like that by the window in the hospital, when she was telephoning Katerina to tell her Vladimir was ill. It was with true sincerity that she said: "I love Vladimir", because she was convinced that it really was the case. She goes into a church and lights a candle for his recovery! All that is truly sincere. It's simply that emotions are by no means all that there is to the individual, emotions do not cost anything. In actual fact something quite different lies hidden within us.

KG: And what's that?

AZ: It seems that a person only appears in his true colours, when someone treads on his toes. It is enough to tread on his sore spot and then all masks fall away, his whole veneer of humanistic values can evaporate in an instant. An individual can lash out at a moment's notice, in complete sincerity. That is, if you like, the terrible *'fleur du mal'* of the 20th century – a century which passed into history without having told us anything new about the old myths, about how good wins out in the end and evil will be punished. Nothing about Auschwitz, the Gulag or what is happening in the whole of our legal system – the whole of that never-ending nightmare. Today the whole world knows the names of Magnitsky's[55] killers, even what they look like – but it's unlikely to change anything. After the 20th century, the 21st is continuing to bear fruit in the same vein: telling us the same terrible fairy-tale about the human race. I am not sure that Dostoevsky, if he had known what we know today, would have written about Raskolnikov's repentance, for example. Crime *without* Punishment is what the real world is offering. The 20th century

---

[55] Sergei Magnitsky – a Russian lawyer involved in a high profile anti-corruption case, who later died in prison after inhumane treatment at the hands of guards.

brought us a new myth to the effect that evil is not punished and that it is slumbering in any one of us, even the most ordinary of human beings. That's what I mean when I say that the world resembles 'Elena's state'.

I even conducted an experiment. I cut out a large part of the dialogue about the will, leaving in only the beginning and end of the scene, starting with Vladimir's announcement about the will and going as far as the moment when Elena bursts out with accusations. From the stage when she is almost flirting with Vladimir ("I don't even want to listen" – with reference to the will) to the moment when Vladimir 'touches a raw nerve'. I saw how a person could change completely in the course of a mere three minutes. Yet a person could not become someone quite different so fast. He will always have been that other person as well. I suddenly realised that the potential for what came over Elena later on – the ability to kill – had always been a part of her. That narrow way of looking at things, when out of fear she starts interpreting everything going on around her as part of her own failure. Her feminine capacity for flirting is the surface: deep down she was already a different person. We deliberately 'started the count-down'. Her mental activity is contained within tight boundaries, as it were, and she is no longer lying to herself. At last, Elena's invisible face comes to the fore – as if shown up in an X-ray. Her crime is a snapshot of the real Elena. It is very important to appreciate that she has assumed the role of the main interpreter of Vladimir's words: it is precisely she who chooses to read into his words a threat to her family's very survival. Elena no longer seems to hear what Vladimir is saying to her. If she had had the intelligence or the time, Elena might well have assessed the situation differently. After all he says to her that she will have an annuity for the rest of her life. "Every month till the end of your days you will receive money, which will, I assure you, be sufficient." Why shouldn't she believe him? Perhaps it will be enough for her to support her family as well? After all, it is Vladimir's right to determine the fate of his fortune. But to continue... It is only in the light of Elena's blind love for her grandson and her son that everything looks terrible. It's not as if anything irrevocable, extraordinary or inexorably disastrous would happen if her grandson Sasha were suddenly to end up in the army, would it? Elena's love, like a mica window, stops her seeing reality clearly. She does not see what kind of person her son is – a banal parasite. It is obvious to Vladimir: a single encounter was probably enough for him to realise what kind of person Sergei was. He would not have allowed Sergei across his threshold even. What's more he demands from Elena that she should not drag them all into his life. "We had an understanding that I live with you and not with your relatives." He is also well aware of what the situation is regarding Elena's grandson. When we held auditions various people came along, telling us their own and others' stories. People in their sixties or seventies, by no means Vladimirs as far as their incomes or fortunes were concerned. Yet they too brought me actual examples of similar situations. For fourteen years a man and his wife had been living in the wife's two-room flat, but there was a stepson as well, aged 25. Sometimes he "would not emerge from his dark room for days on end. He wouldn't even let anyone come into the room. What was he up to in there? He would come out to eat, put his plate in the sink and then go back again". They would tell him: "The parquet near the door of your room has come adrift, you need to fix it back." He would simply reply: "It's you that want it fixed, fix it." Vladimir was well aware of what Sasha and Sergei were like. With regard to Sergei he says: "You need to take steps to make sure he tries to find a way out himself." Vladimir's actions and opinions are well-founded. Someone even suggested that he had arranged monthly annuity payments for Elena precisely because she would simply have poured all the money into her good-for-nothing family and it would have gone up in smoke. Vladimir behaved sensibly and, if we were to stretch a point, we might even say humanely, because that sensible decision stemmed from his concern for Elena's future. Elena's logic is simple in the extreme, as clear as a bell: "Oh dear! Sasha will come a cropper and – Oh horrors! – they'll send him off to Ossetia...".

KG: The way you see things, a person has a level of emotions, in which he himself believes and in an utterly sincere way, and then another deeper level of 'feelings' that stretch further back in time and are more powerful – feelings of which a person is not even aware. Yet at moments of emotional crisis they surface of their own accord. Those feelings are the kind which can set horrific events in motion. Because you leave room for a future surge of those feelings, your characters are not truly 'emotional' and you can tell nothing from their faces. A character is more than the sum of his emotions, than his everyday behaviour, than his own perception of himself. The camera sees in him what he does not see in himself – what we call the 'Elena state'.

AZ: Or an apocalypse, which actually means 'revelation', i.e. the unfolding of the terrible last truth – where the invisible becomes visible, where the deepest depth is stripped bare, where everything comes to an end. In this respect the scene between Vladimir and Katerina is an interesting one. It is like a death-bed scene. Who is Katerina for him? Is she more than just his 'seed'? It is precisely Katerina who sets the action moving. On encountering her for the first time after a long interval, Vladimir realises that there have been enough lies, that he should put a stop to the convenient untruth which he had created for himself. Katerina is his Cordelia, his true daughter. Indeed when Elena says to Katerina "now be gentler with him", that is almost a direct quote from King Lear. That is what Goneril and Regan say. Elena is used to living a ritual, complete with ritual feelings, including her real attachment – not to Vladimir, but to her son. Katerina's words stop Elena and her lies in their tracks. She also starts out by talking in an abrupt tone with Vladimir: "There's no meaning anywhere". She can hardly be seen when she says that, because she is standing against the light. When Katerina draws nearer to him. Vladimir can see her more clearly, then it becomes even easier to understand and in the end Katerina, despite everything, makes it clear to him what really does have meaning – simply his own love for her, the fact that they, father and daughter, really love each other, and this is for real.

KG: In this sense Katerina is an angel of redemption appearing to the ill man without mercy, with a truncheon and a full-on attack?

AZ: Yes, perhaps that's it. She brings tragedy into the action, because Vladimir decides to opt for her. When it comes to love between him and Elena, there cannot be any such thing: their love has been 'discredited'. Both of them realise that. Their relationship is a contractual one, convenient for both of them and they both use each other. It is possible that in the beginning, ten years earlier, emotion had stirred, something more sincere, yet even then it had already been undermined, there was already a touch of decay about it. The world of this over-age couple is a loveless one, although each person in the relationship requires love. The husband requires that his wife should attend to all his needs, should keep everything clean and tidy, for she is in a position to create an ideal domestic setting for him.

KG: While Elena sees love as Vladimir keeping her family.

AZ: Yes, it is a typically Russian situation. Foreigners sometimes ask me: "Is it true that in your country women are little more than servants, with no real rights?" I reply: "For the most part, yes. We are still Asians in this respect. A patriarchal way of life is something very Russian." Both our men and women go along with that. They call domestic servicing 'love'.

KG: Do you really regard all that as a Russian phenomenon?

AZ: Now I'll start contradicting myself again. No, not really. Many people who have seen *Elena* understand that properly. One of them said to me: "Everything is fine, I understand it all, the subtle acting skill, but if you were to take the characters and transfer them to another world and call her Hannah and him Hans, nothing would change. Or even to Italy." This film-goer was talking about the universal nature of the film – seeing it as a minus. Asking as it were, where there was something of ours, something Russian? Suggesting we add some feelings, some panache and some 'verve'. I see that aspect of the film as a plus. I even thought previously that as the film was deeply embedded in our environment, it would require explanation in an international context. Yet it turned out in that very context no questions were asked, as if people never wondered: "Are things with you in Russia really like that?" Indeed, in Salonika, in Greece people even said to me: "That's all about us, that's how we live. It's a precise portrait of our society. There are Sergeis here too – everywhere. In the birthplace of tragedy the same flowers are growing." When people in Russia say to me: "That's not about us. Where are our salted cucumbers? Where are the sausages and vodka?

Where are our people spoiling for a fight?" I reply that I had wanted deliberately to leave behind all the insistence on straightforward emotional content, which is so simple to reproduce. I even rejected the typical theatrical device of getting the actors to play their parts in the light of those events which are going to shape the *whole* play, when you drag along the chain of events from start to finish, as it were. I was so keen to avoid doing so that I did not let any of the actors with minor parts read the whole script in advance. They had no idea of what was going on between Vladimir and Elena. Katerina, for example, did not know that her father had been murdered – I don't mean Katerina of course, but the actress Elena Lyadova and, when she was preparing for the part, she quite naturally noted the sequence of her scenes as (1) In the hospital and (2) Funeral. For her, Vladimir had simply died in hospital from a heart attack. It was in that state of limited knowledge that she had acted the part. The cinema provides different opportunities from those of the stage: it offers fragmentation, more clear space and freedom. The resulting lack of knowledge can sometimes have considerable impact. The 'ignorance' means that an actor is present precisely within his given situation, selects precisely the right note and when different actors' notes and situations clash, this makes the film as a whole more dramatic. That's how I see it.

Andrey Smirnov commented to me: "You keep an actor lying in bed for five whole minutes. Without any change in the setting. Nobody's going to watch that (the conversation with Katerina in the hospital). It's impossible to sit it out!" I replied: "Let's risk it. For some reason I'm sure that people will see the scene out." In the end we had three whole scenes like that in the film which lasted for five minutes plus. What's more, in two of them Smirnov is lying in bed from start to finish!... On an ordinary day you usually film two to three minutes of usable footage. When it came to the scene in the hospital (as in the two others) we turned the camera on and, for the whole five and a half minutes, we filmed Katerina and then we shifted the camera round and Andrey Smirnov was filmed for the full five minutes. The scene turned out detailed, relaxed and indeed unusually long for today's cinema. Three long scenes with dialogue in a film like that with almost no action is a lot. So this approach, without fragmentation is bound to help an actor be genuine, as I see it. That's because the only thing required of an actor at moments like that is to be absolutely genuine. Absorbed in that particular day, in that particular scene. No future prospects or long-range tasks. A shot in a film is our here-and-now every time, while the whole is created using different means...

KG: And how did Elena first appear to *you*? What made you realise that this was the 'real thing'. It was after all just an incident from the life of the scriptwriter, Oleg Negin...

AZ: Not exactly... Although Oleg's father had indeed died about a year previously, he had not been living with Oleg's mother for some time at that stage and had taken up with a quite different woman. Then at the wake after his father's funeral – he had not been an old or sick man when he died – Oleg's relatives started gossiping: "It's strange that your father died and then for some reason that new wife, a complete outsider, and not you took the decision for him to be cremated. It's not at all clear what was behind it..." They started winding him up and in that 'wound-up' state he started imagining things and imagined this story with the perfect murder – a story which, of course, has nothing to do with real events.

KG: What drew you into the story in the first place, what got you hooked?

AZ: As always, it was most unusual. I was even taken aback somewhat. Then I re-read the episode where Elena gives Vladimir the Viagra pills together with his heart medication and paces to and fro outside the closed door, which she later opens, only to discover Vladimir in his death throes. Oleg Negin is very precise in his descriptions, utterly realistic. Indeed, he knows a great deal about bodies and anatomy, about that whole domain. In the script it says "Vladimir passes wind" and I thought it had to mean something like 'pass away'. Later Oleg said to me "Pass as in 'pass wind'. Did you think I meant he was passing to another, heavenly world, using some kind of euphemism for death? No! I literally mean that there was an unpleasant smell in the room." I was really stunned: it was a real lurching back into a dry report and physical detail and I couldn't shake off my surprise for a long time. It turns out that death is not something dignified and clean as portrayed in films, but rather different. That physiological honesty impressed me from the very first reading and it would seem that precisely that honesty lent the film its narrative tone – the convincing realistic detail drawn from everyday life. That was the doorway through which I stepped into the *Elena* theme. What is all the stranger and more surprising is that the death scene did not end up as part of the film. Until the very end, right up until editing started, I was convinced that it had to be included. We even did a large number of takes of the death-throes. On that particular day we had a medical consultant on set, who had observed death on several occasions in the course of his practice. Later I came to realise that it should not be in the final version. What I had found moving in literature would be achieved on screen via different means. In the current version Elena simply hands her husband the tablets, he swallows them, she closes the bedroom door and then waits before opening it again to find him dead. That's all.

Negin's phrase is a tuning fork for the terrible truth, when the word 'pass' loses its lofty ring. In my mind that sentence was to become the basis from which the rest of the film's narrative found its way forward. Not a path that was 'aesthetic' or 'beautiful' but a very austere, straight path – 'aesthetic' only as a document. There are no allusions, no symbols, no poetic images. It is a precise, genuine story drawn from ordinary life. The simpler and more 'ordinary' it appears, the more impact it will have. Long before this film was shot, a film-goer said to me: "Now we'll be expecting your Elena the Beautiful": she was probably expecting a continuation of the aesthetic approach to be found in *The Return* and *The Banishment*. My spontaneous answer at the time had been: "That would be a long wait. It's going to be Elena the Horrible." That was not so much a concept for the film-to-be, but more of an assumption about the state the audience would be in after watching *Elena*...

KG: Tell me, how did you all achieve that pervasive atmosphere of suspense which permeates the film from the very beginning? It all begins like Hitchcock's *The Birds* with a crow looking into the window of a flat.

THREE INTERVIEWS. QUESTIONS TO THE DIRECTOR

AZ: I shall have to disappoint you. We did not set out deliberately to create any kind of atmosphere. Yes, the first shot is of a crow, but that is an easily recognisable, everyday part of Moscow. In the studio where we were putting the finishing touches to the script – in the Old Arbat district – there were crows cawing loudly all day long outside the windows of the little basement where I was sitting. We made two versions of the opening shot. In the first place, I wasn't sure it wouldn't be 'laying it on too thick'. On top of that I wasn't sure it would turn out well, that the crow would fly on to the necessary branch as required. So, to start with, we just did some takes of sunrise without any crows. Yet after a trained crow had twice flown to the required spot, right into the middle of the shot, into the cross-hairs, I decided to leave that as part of the film. It is not any kind of omen, although many people read that into it. I realised that it would have that impact but do not insist that it has to be interpreted like that and only that. A crow is, of course, a fairy-tale character, a harbinger of death, war and misfortune, heralding dire events, but at the same time that bird is also just an ordinary Moscow resident. What was more important was capturing the start of the day. Life is stirring, there is the chirping of waking birds. First one, then another. The crows are cawing – they are the first to stir and then come the sparrows. The shadows disperse and a new day begins. A tram clatters in the distance. Someone outside must have bumped into a car, setting off an alarm. A door slams and then a car moves off. Noises familiar to all of us. It was the same in the flat. First all is quiet with everyone sleeping. Then everything starts gently to move. Elena has woken up and gradually comes to. She begins moving about the flat, opening the blinds: the coffee-grinder starts to hum and the television set comes to life. Life gradually gathers pace. Then Elena wakes Vladimir and he emerges for breakfast: sounds, sounds and more sounds and not until the eighth minute of silence does the first dialogue begin. Life has started out of nothing. The sun has come up, the curtain is raised and we have begun to observe a story. Incidentally, if all the dialogues from this script are put together and read through, we end up with an extremely simple and clear story. It's minimal. Everything is announced right from the start: the money, son Sergei, daughter Katerina. All the seeds of the action are sown in that very first dialogue. The other strands of the tune – as in a work of music – serve merely to develop the main theme, to expand the central collision so as to set the spring of the drama in motion. It was so dense and concentrated, so transparent and single-track that the minimalist diagram had to be diluted, supplied with pauses and gaps, various moods and atmospheres, which tell of other things not to be found in the path of the main narrative.

KG: Essentially, the whole film is a single day. It begins in the morning and ends in the evening. There may be fragments of several different days, but when collected together it makes up just one day.

AZ: Yes, it presents as a rondo. First a blanket of total darkness, then a ray of light appears, the trees start to sway and the birds wake up. Conflicts are mapped out and the balance of power is made clear. When Elena comes into Sergei's flat for the first time the audience simply gasped – I was told about that once. The contrast was too great. There had been a hi-tech flat, where one would not even expect people to speak Russian, and then suddenly – our Biryulovo, our reality – side by side, in a single moment. The longer it goes on, the more contrasts there are: Vladimir's daughter who does not want children on the one hand and Elena's highly fertile relatives on the other. And conflicts all the way. The contrasts are extreme. It is a completely polarised world. Each extreme serves to underline the other, contrasting and balancing, highlighting and making us feel that there cannot be any other kind of world. In this black cosmic darkness, under the raised curtain, what passes before us is a whole world condensed into the story of two households, two families. Just as you find in myths which always present two extremes. Then in the finale, when we are reaching the point of an irrevocable decision, when these two worlds come together at the moment of the murder, from that point on everything is moving towards conciliation and fading away. From a state of peace and back again to peace once more. The rondo has come full circle. Evening, a family supper, twilight, branches of trees, under the bark of which the sap of life is flowing. That is all. Then the light will go out, without giving us hope or anything else, simply after telling us yet another horror story from our world of horrors. A world where there has been an Auschwitz and a Gulag; a world in which the files on Magnitsky and

Politkovskaya[56] will be buried for ever; a world in which the myth insisting that evil will be punished without fail has reached the stage where it has to be re-examined; a world where evil can turn up in your house with the everyday banality of a plumber. That was the only way we, who made this film, could proceed in the world of that amiable fellow from the television who had murdered his mother.

KG: Yet the actual shape of the world you created is magnificent. Hence the 'cosmic' feel about it. It inhabits the cosmos and its rhythms, it is suspended within it. Elena is another name for beauty or the cosmos – in Greek it means 'adornment'. The actress herself is splendid, reminiscent of the ancient world. Even the slum blocks on the fringe of the city, where Sergei lives. They are shown in tones of gentle blue, like a watery Venice, like an enormous blue ship destined to carry the whole of mankind. There is no black bleakness. It really is the 'story of the Fall' of our world in the course of a single day, from its creation right to the end, despite the fact that it remains a creation, a work of God's art, and remains splendid. And evil comes to pass invisibly, squeezing through the cracks. The harsh, everyday dimension unfolds like a poisoned flower above the inner powers of the cosmos. In this sense, the question as to the nature of Evil assumes great importance. What is it really? After all, murder, theft and so on are only external forms of evil. Insignificant, laughable ones. The essence of evil is spiritual. In this sense as well perhaps we shall find an answer as to why you did not show the scene of Vladimir's death. Perhaps because that is not where evil is to be found. As I see it, evil lies not in the death itself and not even in the fact that Elena gives Vladimir tablets that are incompatible with life. All that is actually shown in an extremely sterile, clinical way. Elena does not kill him with a knife, she lets Vladimir kill himself. And he does not know that he is doing the killing. The crux of the crime involves no flesh, nothing substantial. Even the tablets are not passed from hand to hand. The murder is a perfect one in the sense that it is absolutely 'theoretical': it is carried out in accordance with a medical manual.

---

[56] Anna Politkovskaya – a well-known Russian journalist, writer and human rights activist, strongly opposed to the Chechen war and who exposed human tights abuses there. She was gunned down and killed in the lift of her block of flats in 2006.

It is a murder effected through knowledge. Yet we in the audience also only have knowledge about it and that knowledge has nowhere to focus. What will serve as its expression, as its very own emblem? An emblem of evil? And so, in my view, the most important shot in the film is one shot from above: Elena's younger grandson, sleeping just in a nappy on the bed of the murdered Vladimir, on the same dark and expensive bedspread. The child sleeps, the innocent sleeps, but the audience beholds him in horror. He is the latest offshoot, the 'seed'. When he stirs and pulls himself up on all fours, he already appears as a monster. This is the vision of evil and it is Elena's sin. This child does not serve as the justification for anything, he is shown as Evil. It is an infernal vision, definitely not a divine one. This very spot is where the crime is committed, where the world fell. This is where someone ceased to exist. This I feel is what appears in the black square that you saw as you embarked upon the theme of *Elena*.

AZ: I'm glad that you saw it like that...

THERE ARE NO SYMBOLS HERE[57]

Question: I know that directors do not like this kind of question but I have seen your film *The Return*, which I enjoyed very much. I felt that everything in it was clear for me, that I understood what it was about. But when I began to read your book, I realised that I had not understood even 10% of it. So, during this discussion, what I should like to understand most of all is what *Elena* is about. Possibly we only think we have understood what it's about. There are bound to be plenty of meanings in it which we did not consider.

Andrey Zvyagintsev: You were right to note that no director likes being asked what his film is about because, if that question were an easy one to answer, what would have been the point of making it in the first place? Godard put it even more bluntly: "Why make a film if the script has been written? There it is finished, lying on the table, why shoot anything." That's what led him to say that he went out on to the set with just one sheet of paper on which was written: "He goes up to her from the left, she looks up, he says this and that." So let's go about it like this: if suddenly in the course of this gathering, some urgent question arises like the one we're talking about now, I shall try and resolve it somehow, but I don't think it's right to start out with that.

---

[57] This text has been compiled from two discussions about the film *Elena*. The first took place in the 'Mir Iskusstva' (World of Art) cinema on December 14, 2011 as part of the 'Artery Cinema' project and was published by World of Art Publishers as a separate brochure in September 2012. The second discussion with the title 'There are no symbols here' was published in the journal *Iskusstvo kino* (Art of Cinema) and is the recorded text of a master-class held on March 21, 2011 in the Institute of Contemporary Art in Moscow.

Question: It's interesting that you should mention Godard, the director who basically initiated the Nouvelle Vague in France. Do you see yourself as one of his successors?

AZ: No, I merely recalled his words by chance.

Question: It turned out very much to the point. In actual fact I wanted to ask: do you feel sorry for the characters who are going to be living in that flat after Vladimir? Don't they feel alien to you personally? It seemed to me that you passed sentence on them unequivocally...

AZ: I thought that the conversation centring on Elena would be difficult. My relationship to those characters is... we-ell...

Voice from the audience: ...made clear.

AZ: Clear? Do you think so? (He smiles) To be honest, I don't really understand myself whether it's clear or not, because I was born into that world. For many years I lived in a similar setting: a Khrushchev-era flat with my mother in what you could, I suppose, call poverty. I did not inherit any fortune or title. You should never spit into a shared well or at your own fellow-citizens, people who live next to you. You simply don't do that! Although, of course, there's plenty to discuss on that subject in the film. Vladimir in relation to Elena, Katerina in relation to Sergei and Tatiana and then Sasha with his gang-mates. If you follow that graph, it's naturally going to take you right down to the bottom. That's obvious.

Question: Do you just think that about the characters in the film or about society in general?

AZ: Possibly... That's possibly my view not just of our characters but – subconsciously – of our society as a whole. A sense of entropy permeates it all. It's as if we are losing some important ability, which could hold everything together and keep in place the experience passed down through generations, stop everything sliding downwards.

On December 10th, when people came out onto Bolotnaya Square[58], there was a feeling that some new layer of thought was taking shape or simply being preserved as a permanent entity perhaps. On the 10th of December those people were looking each other in the eye: it was as if they had recognised that 'there are people like us' and that their numbers were not so small after all. That was, in my view, the most important thing that happened on December 10th. It's clear, of course, that unfortunately nothing's going to change: there will be new 'presidents', but they will just go on doing the same as before. Have a look at the film *The Ides of March*[59]: it's all shown clearly there in an accomplished and exhaustive account.

Question: And did you include any message for those in power in your film?

AZ: I have to confess I didn't. It seems to me that they live on another planet, as it were. Sometimes you grasp all too clearly that there is absolutely no point in counting on any kind of feedback. Yet, to be honest, I don't think this state of affairs can last forever.

Voice from the audience: They don't see when they're slipped Viagra, they really don't see.

AZ: You mean like Vladimir?...

Question: Leaving names to one side, but there is something worth noticing in that isn't there?

AZ: Of course, it's not just a question of names, although Vladimir is a name pregnant with meaning – 'master of the world'. It's clear that he's a real patriarch, father of the people, in charge of the situation

---

[58] Bolotnaya Square – a square in central Moscow where the major protests against the Russian presidential elections of 2012 were held. The location is strongly associated with liberal, anti-government protests and the 'white ribbon' movement.

[59] *The Ides of March* (2011) – a political drama film directed by George Clooney.

and so on.

Voice from the audience: Who loves his misguided people.

AZ: He scolds the people and showers it with moral admonitions. You see how interesting it is? Now you'll understand what I was getting at, when we started this conversation. It's best not to ask me what this film is about. I would have said to you: "We made a film about..." and then your own vision of it would have evaporated. A film comes into being in the minds of those watching it. That is where it takes shape with all its implications and subtexts, with all its additional nuances. Let's say that for me the centre of the film is Elena. What's most important is what happens to her soul, to her, but most of the journalists who have seen the film protest that it's about something quite different! They exclaim: "How wonderful that you've grappled with social issues!" And that simply fills me with horror. But I'm not going to chase after each one of them and say: "That wasn't what I was filming! Look around you, change your angle!" Because, once a film has been shot, its life from then on is no longer within the director's control, just as a child's life comes to elude its parents' control. All I can do by then is seek consolation from the thoughts of great men on this subject... Oscar Wilde, for instance, said that art was a mirror reflecting the person looking into it, not real life at all. There is another saying on the subject as well: "Not only do we watch films, but they watch us." That's really to the point as well because, when all is said and done, our aim when making films is not to express ourselves, but to prompt others to think, see and understand. Nobody – not even the director – can say what a film means. All the meanings which manifest themselves over and above the planned one, the 'contraband' ones, are a precious acquisition. That's what enables the cinema to stay alive.

Question: If we turn to your own creative process, the script for instance and what you finished up with in the end – do you feel that they are far apart? Does the finished product differ substantially from what you had in mind originally?

AZ: I read in the writings of some director or other that "a film is always a plan minus the lost pieces." I think, however, that films can fortunately make new acquisitions along the way as well.

In November, for instance, we were looking for an outside location in Molochny Lane, trying to decide where to set up the camera. Later our location-manager spent three whole months trying to get some kind of response, to obtain leave to film there at all, until I eventually complained to Rodnyansky. The very next day permission to film there came through. While we were walking around there, looking for a place to set up the cameras, suddenly we saw a file of migrant workers walking past, ten of them. It was pure chance, but first-rate: straight off the street towards us.

Question: Migrant workers right next to Vladimir's block of flats – surely that was no coincidence? Didn't you plan them?

AZ: That idea was not in the script till November. But once we'd seen them, we realised straightway that they were part of the film. We didn't grab the moment, of course, and do a bit of extra filming there and then – in the film you see a group scene with extras made up. Shooting it was planned and included in the schedule in advance. You need to understand, a film will have had a long period of gestation: the actual filming is not the script any more, but neither is it the film. It is a magnet, a centre of attraction. It begins to draw things in, turning them from mere coincidences into signs. We try not to let slip through the net what comes knocking, what presents itself.

Question: Like messengers from the reality which you are just starting to create.

AZ: Yes, if you wish – like messengers.

Question: Tell me – what about the remarkable dialogue between Katerina and her father – was that in the script or did you make changes in it as you went along?

AZ: The dialogue between Katerina and her father in the hospital had been completed by Oleg and it was amended during the process of filming, but in a completely natural way. When you have already been immersed in a text for a long time and know every twist in it, the actors start coming to rehearsals and working with the text and you suddenly realise that something might be superfluous, while in another place something might need adding. For example, some extra phrases were added to the dialogue between Vladimir and Elena in the scene which he opens with the words: "I've read your note." One remark of Vladimir's in that conversation is very important in my opinion: "If it was a question of the boy's health, God forbid, of course I wouldn't hesitate. The money would be on the table tomorrow." That remark appeared later on, it badly needed to be added, because the tone of that scene had been very dry and harsh. For Elena the army is a horrific prospect and Sasha is bound to get shot if he joins up. Vladimir might well have objected: "The whole population serves in it. What of it? Let him serve as well." Here we have two very different views of one and the same thing: for Elena the army means death, while for Vladimir it's just part of the normal order of things. There was another phrase which badly needed to be added to the dialogue: "I hope you're not taking money out of your account for them?" The phrase "I live with you, not with your relatives" and Vladimir's explanation of hedonism: "Selfish is what you'd say" also came into being during rehearsals with the actors. That kind of thing injects life into a script. You go into episodes in more detail and start to understand where things are missing and where things need reducing.

    Then there's an example with Elena Lyadova – Katerina. She also came out with a sentence which made its way into the film completely by chance, which I think is pure magic. In the scene with the lawyer – a long static one, consisting mainly of conversation – we began by filming him. I don't remember exactly how many takes we did but, by about the sixth, the actor had managed the whole scene splendidly. Then we turned the camera on to Markina and completed a number of long takes with her as well. Prior to that we had spent a whole morning on a number of long and fairly tricky takes with the young secretary who brings in the coffee. Towards the end of the working day, we at last turned the camera on Lyadova. For an actor, a moment like that is psychologically difficult: you've been on set the whole day, taking part in the scene with the others, languishing on your chair and waiting and then the camera turns to you and you're not really ready after all, worn out, exhausted. It's difficult to convey that state but I know something about it from personal experience. In the script the episode finished with her saying: "That's all clear then." That was in response to Elena saying in connection with the money in the safe: "I've already checked and there's nothing there." The editing after that should have provided an immediate transition to the film's next episode. Then, so as to break up the shape of the scene, which had bored us silly over the course of the day, and introduce something spontaneous, or new perhaps, I said to her: "Lena, now get up from your chair as if to stretch your legs. The lawyer will react, saying it would be better to finish there and then and you, in reply, can say something to the effect that you'd rather continue. Somehow we'll splice it all together."

Everyone took up their positions and we started shooting. Lena stood up, walked round her chair, leant against the back of it, while the lawyer could be heard saying off screen: "If you want we can stop now and continue later, on another day if you like." Lena came back with: "No, no – why should we? Let's round it off today. Don't you think so, Elena Anatolievna?" Markina responded spontaneously: "Yes, yes. Make it today." Then there was a pause and Lyadova was waiting for me to say: "Cut!" I was perfectly happy with it all and I knew there was still quite a bit of film left in the camera. Then suddenly she came out with the magical: "Well and how are we going to carve up the house?" The lawyer suddenly took up the phrase and, in just the right tone, he said: "We shall carve it up by the book!" It's hard to believe, but the whole of that ending was pure improvisation.

Question: Did situations arise in which you added things to the script as you were going along or changed things radically?

AZ: There were no instances of radical changes, but during work on the director's script new ideas could always crop up or even whole episodes. In particular, the episode in the church, the episode with the horse and the whole ending of the film were introduced at a later stage. In the first version of the script the end had been different, but we had all felt convinced that an ending with a real impact would emerge. A more powerful one, if we can put it like that. We could have kept to the ending in the script, but we were after something rather different.

Question: What kind of ending was originally planned?

AZ: The script finished on the landing where Sergei and his neighbour had been working out what had happened with the electricity supply. During their short conversation the light on the landing came back on and, after taking their leave of each other, the neighbours returned to their respective flats. The camera-man and I lingered on the empty landing and watched the electricity meter start to revolve again, counting out its kilowatts, just as life is renewed and spins on regardless. So not long before we filmed it, we came up with the idea of an ending with a fight, the episode with 'Sasha's little world', with his "Give us a beer!" and the violence in the wood. All the scenes from that point on and right up until the final credits came into being much later than the rest, some three or four months after we had started the filming.

Question: Why did you use another ending?

AZ: You could say that the electricity meter is a metaphor from the world of Sergei, Elena's son. But that is not the last world shown in our film. The last one was not revealed for a long time. It is the world of Elena's grandson, Sasha. We encountered it in a wood, outside civilization on the very edge of human habitation. That was where Sasha, the person for whom Elena committed her crime, lives and hangs out and we moved into that world, so as to follow the character's footsteps to the very end. And the first thing we came across after the unusually static world of Sergei and, indeed, Vladimir as well, was a dynamic fight with no holds barred. There could only have been three outcomes: Option 1 – Sasha gets killed; Option 2 – Sasha kills someone else; Option 3 – nobody kills anybody. The first two possibilities would have brought the film to an end with a fatal outcome, while the third provided space for other opportunities. We moved through the narrow space available once more and, as we did so, we found ourselves back at the windows of Vladimir's flat: we were looking again through the bare branches of the trees at the people inside. We see Elena once again and we see her younger grandson lying now in the very centre of his new world, which Elena has brought to the fledgling 'in her beak'. Now the cycle is complete, now we have seen it all.

Voice from the audience: But an ending like that leaves everything open, in the air.

AZ: Precisely. At some stage during a discussion with members of the public like today's, an image occurred to me, that of a 'closed and open ending'. A closed ending is one where everything is settled beyond any doubt, where evil is punished or clearly about to be. Retribution functions as a mechanism making satisfaction possible. The film comes full circle and is transformed into an elegant globe, inside which its own laws operate, recurrent patterns that are familiar to us. After the crescendo of horrors – murder, lies, theft, forgery, fighting – the people in the audience gasped, held their breath and waited to see what would happen next. If at that moment Sasha had been killed, the film-goer could have heaved a sigh of relief, saying: "Well that's it, the film's clear to me. I know where to file it away. What's the next thing I have planned for today?" Do you see what I mean? But in the situation we used, the audience gasps, holds its breath and then...

Voice from the audience: Happy End!

AZ: No, you haven't realised what I'm getting at. The audience has gasped but has not been given the chance to heave a sigh of relief. It has been left high and dry with an open ending. That's when the film won't let the audience rest, but rather forces everyone to reflect about everything they've seen. If you like, the structure is open-ended in this case – it is not mass production of old ideas and familiar patterns, but a chance for the film-goer to become a co-author involved in the search for meaning.

In general, the film demanded from us a quite different view of events, of crime, of punishment, of human beings. I would call that view 'open' or 'tragic'. I remember talking to Nadezhda Markina, who plays Elena, about how she, as an actress, needed to approach the scene of Vladimir's murder. For an actress that particular episode is an extremely 'rewarding' one, involving a whole range of emotions and six minutes with the character either in close-up or medium close-up. A scene like that provides an actor with a chance to hold the audience transfixed. But to deprive oneself of a vivid emotional immersion in a character costs dear. For both director and actor. It means deciding that inner struggle and acting with emotional light and shade and expressive gestures are all unimportant. Renunciation of that kind is difficult, but it is the only way to move over to a different, sterner register for making sense of what is happening. We are no longer looking out from the inside, from the character's point of view – no, we are taking a view from the outside, we are observing. And when it comes to how an actress decides to play the part, she has to don an impenetrable mask and be aware of herself as a person captive to her own decision and hurtling like a comet to the end.

What we see before us is a rigid trajectory which is straight and clear. There is nothing 'internal'. Everything is *open*. *Revealed*. *Simple*. Simple, intense and terrible. And that is tragedy, profoundly different from a psychological drama.

Question: And how would you describe that difference?

AZ: In my experience – as a film-goer, director, actor – this is what I think. A drama assumes that individuals carry within them both hidden and outwardly displayed plans in various combinations: an individual thinks one thing but manifests through his external appearance something else and that 'truth' needs to come through to the surface in the course of an actor's performance. A drama is always reflection, middle ground, subtext, psychology. That is how a person behaves in real life. He carries within him several meanings, often concealing some of them under a mask. There is nothing criminal about that incidentally, it is simply how living side by side with other people functions. Drama as a genre focuses attention on that feature of human existence. If we take this path, then it would be essential to show doubts, introspection, inner turmoil – the result would have been both 'life-like' and compelling. Drama views life as if through a half-open door: what is inside seeps out and external factors influence internal ones. An actor's performance is showing us all the time the *reasons* why something is taking place.

The tragic view on the other hand is a view that is as wide open as possible. So wide open, so stripped of any sub-text – and this is the paradox – that when we think of famous tragedies, we keep on torturing ourselves by trying to crack the riddle: *why* did what happened happen? We are not given *reasons*. It is simply that in our weakness and, what's more, in retrospect we try to fill what we have seen with a drama of emotions, reasons or psychology: otherwise it is very difficult for us to encompass what has happened. All the same – no reasons are adequate. As Lao Tzu said, "It is only an open door that cannot be broken", namely it is only what is open widest of all that remains more concealed and mysterious than anything else. Therein lies the secret of great tragedies and great *dramatis personae*, like Oedipus, Medea and Orestes. Incidentally in the ancient world actors played their parts in masks! There were no emotions, no innovations in the narrative! All the figures were placed in position in advance: Clytaemnestra, Medea, Oedipus. The spectators knew the story just as well as the author. Emotions and psychological nuances were removed beyond the confines of the acting. Here there were no everyday factors underlying the actor's performance. Violation of divine laws by man (by all of us) or compliance with them is the stuff of tragedy. That is why, if we tried to achieve a conversation at that level, we would be unable to provide a purely dramatic conclusion for the film, answering the question as to *why* one individual killed another. A tragedy is the ultimate burden of horror, compassion, bewilderment, insights, which we are able to experience in response to an individual's deeds or actions, as opposed to his emotions. And none of the reasons we come up with will be enough to explain one simple thing: *Elena decides to kill Vladimir*. In this case the structure of the acting becomes so open, that it can embrace all the meanings and motifs which we (actors, directors, audience) might ascribe to it, but there will never be enough, for our task was to film the fact that one human being *killed* another.

Voice from the audience: Yes, you succeeded in creating the character of Elena which was particularly powerful and not run-of-the-mill, yet this is not a truly 'tragic' character, even as regards the performance of the actress.

AZ: Naturally I realised that it would not be right to take this tragic slant right up to the end. This is being played out on a screen rather than a stage. Also there is a good deal of the everyday in our story. As I was told in Europe, there is even a genre for films like ours – 'kitchen-sink drama'. At first I was taken aback and then, when I started thinking about it, I realised that was apt. All the events take place in the kitchen. Literally. Or at least at a table with unfinished food on it. It is after all a family story. The characters talk over tea or beer and pistachios. This is, of course, why we sought out something in the way of a middle path between tragedy and drama. Especially given that we were working with Nadezhda Markina, in whose case it is very difficult to cut out the psychology: she is a vibrant and very 'organic' actress. For her it would be wrong to move in the direction of pure tragedy, and indeed there was no need for that in *Elena*. It was necessary to find a middle path. Yet that middle path still had to be directed towards the main goal – finding the immobile, fixed point of the key decision, a point round which everything turns.

Question: And do you know where that point is?

AZ: Broadly speaking, yes. It's no secret. After seeing the film twice, a friend of mine said to me that she had picked out the precise moment when Elena takes her decision. She telephones her son Sergei, puts down the receiver and then we see Sergei, who is looking for his beer, and then the whole family starts shelling nuts: after that, editing takes us back to Elena's profile. She is looking out of the window and suddenly the tension falls away: she turns towards the dressing-table, picks something up, raises her eyes – and – looks at herself in the mirror. That's it, that's the point of decision – that 'look into the mirror'.

Question: How long does she sit in front of that mirror?

AZ: Good question. Hard to answer. One of the laws of editing (this I knew as some type of hearsay, but it has since been borne out in practice for me as well) is that the move from one shot to another can take half a second of real time or a week, for example. In real time Elena is probably not sitting there for long. Yet, at the moment when Elena turns her head towards her reflection and, if you remember, raises her eyes and looks hard at herself, there is an instant when – and we tried to do this delicately – there is virtually no sound. Total silence. According to Christian custom, there is a legend telling how the whole world seemed to freeze over, when the infant Jesus was born: the wind stopped rustling in the trees and all the animals – birds, sea creatures and deer, the whole of Nature – stopped in their tracks, but a moment later the wheel of the Universe began to turn again as usual. I found that image fascinating and I thought there might be a parallel here: a moment when a person's choice takes shape, a decision which will determine the whole of that person's future, a point when everything is still possible and when in the heart of that person there are two principles, one of which is going to gain the upper hand. It is in total silence of that kind that the individual chooses his path. In that fragment of the film there is, indeed, virtually no sound. Elena looks at herself in stillness devoid of movement. It seems to me that it is precisely at this point that Elena takes her fateful decision. There is no more introspection after that at all. She moves quickly into Vladimir's study, where she finds a medication manual on a bookshelf – in the past she'd had some kind of medical training – and checks out contraindications. Something Elena had assumed is duly confirmed and after that it's plain sailing. Everything that went before, all the lead-in was for the sake of that one moment of silence, that one glance in the mirror. That's real minimalism, if you like.

Voice from the audience: Yet for that one glance to 'convey its message' with real impact, it has to be prepared. There has to be the 'lead-in' as you said.

AZ: As I see it, all the necessary things for that are in place. First of all we narrow the flow of time prior to that moment – 'now or never'. Elena finds herself in a situation, where she has no time at all in which to take a careful, informed decision. If you remember Vladimir says: "Tomorrow morning the lawyer's coming round. I want to do a draft version of my will." The scriptwriters who put those words into his mouth were underlining that this was going to happen 'tomorrow morning'. And now, when he actually says those words, it is already after lunch, so Elena has no time at all to weigh up everything carefully, to consider what's involved, to cool down and think. In addition, let me remind you of the words we hear in the dialogue between Elena and Sergei on the telephone a few seconds before she takes that look in the mirror. Incidentally, that dialogue came into being when Oleg and I were already sitting working at the director's script and there were two practical reasons for adding it. In the first place it was a question of the general rhythm of the film: we needed to be in Sergei's space again, albeit for not very long. The second reason (and I don't really know how to put it) was that, if we needed to collect together at a single table all the reasons weighting the scales for Elena, we, the audience, needed to look carefully at Elena's whole family in pregnant silence, so as to sense what we could perhaps call their 'despair'. And how might Sergei's space be incorporated naturally into the story at that particular point? We had to have a reason to move there and that was why we thought up that conversation. So Elena telephones Sergei and, in that dialogue, if you remember, she says: "I do think... there's some truth in what he says." In other words Elena agrees that Vladimir's point of view is, broadly speaking, the right one. She says that, puts down the receiver and we are transferred straightaway to Sergei's world. While Elena has three mirrors round her dressing-table, three Elenas, Sergei has his own 'Trinity' sitting round the table shelling nuts. Each person making up the threesome has his Holy Grail. Then we return to Elena, into her space in front of the mirror – to that key moment, the moment of decision, the moment where this character is stripped bare and where the outer space around her is reduced to a minimum. At that moment the actress does not need to act any more. She just has to *be* the person staring into the mirror.

So, on returning to what was there previously, if we had shown in detail on the screen the doubts Elena was experiencing, her emotional anguish as she took her decision, all we would actually have done is underline the fact that decisions like that are taken with difficulty. That's all there is to it. Ideas which are familiar to everyone and even banal – no more than that. It's not as if the idea that killing someone is wrong would explain anything. Would it have been worth making a film just to say that? The film is being made to convey more terrible things. For example that such a decision was taken with little effort.

One glance in the mirror and that was all. Murder as a state of mind, an extreme event and tantamount to killing yourself. *Those* were the kind of implications which we hoped to bring out.

Voice from the audience: I have heard many opinions about the film *Elena* and people often say that your characters are negative. That is how you portray them...

AZ: ...so that they appear 'negative' to some people? What to say in reply? The very terminology has an air of mothballs about it. In everyday life there are no positive or negative people around us. From one day to the next someone you've viewed as negative will all of a sudden turn out to be not such a bad fellow after all. It's all subjective. A man's character manifests itself in his actions.

I am not a fan of models like the following: you take up a script, notice a 'positive' character in it and start emphasising all his charming aspects and hiding away or toning down anything that might be 'negative'. Moves like that are too simple, even if "after adding drama and psychology" you start introducing something 'negative' into the good character and something 'positive' into the bad one. As I see it, if dramatic art is to advance, clichés of that kind have to be avoided. What's the point of them? To create 'positive' characters so that young lads start wearing their baseball caps back-to-front, like their favourite screen heroes? That's an infantile way of looking at the world. A person sitting in the cinema – and the same applies to me too as a film-goer – needs to see an objective picture of the world, how that world is arranged, what kind of decisions people take, to look at the choices people make, at what determines those choices and ask himself: "Doesn't that apply to me as well?" To watch a film like that always requires 'work'. When that 'work' is over, without hardly noticing it we are compelled to begin looking for meaning – not in the characters themselves, who have presented us with a particular story of some kind, but in ourselves and the closer we look into ourselves, the more unexpected the answers will be that we can find with regard to the film. The characters are only conductors, only mirrors. In Smolensk one film-goer asked me: "What is the educational function of your film?" There is no such function. I do not create positive characters to be imitated. I am concerned with other things. I try to open up questions to the audience, open up one door after another, not suffocate them with answers. If what I do also creates opportunities for developing aesthetic taste I consider my task to have been completed in full.

Question: I came to a modest assumption that in your film there are more parallels with *The Brothers Karamazov* than with *Crime and Punishment*. I am now referring to the dialogue between Ivan Karamazov and Smerdyakov, about the position of Ivan Karamazov. The idea that if there is no God, then everything is permitted. In the last dialogue between Elena and her husband, Vladimir's position is that there is no such thing as equality, might is right and there is no God and in reply to that there is the position of a simple Russian woman, Elena, who is not familiar with any such terms and who responds through action. When all is said and done, they got their just deserts: Vladimir tells her that there is no such thing as God and that he is strong, while Elena responds by concluding that she can behave towards him in whatever way she sees fit.

AZ: A fine idea! Far from just a modest assumption. I like the way you *look* in that direction. Only it is clear that Elena as a character does not move on directly from those thoughts: "Oh, so there's no God, you tell me! So I shall hurl a hand-grenade at you, you fascist!" The issue is of course a much wider one. The question of God's 'non-being' à la Heidegger arises, which we sense like some kind of 'climate'. Elena's actions and ways of looking at the world (or to take a wider view – how she sees the individual in the modern world) are dictated by the state of the spiritual climate she finds herself in, one of emptiness devoid of any moral sustenance or any meaningful belief that could be central to her life. The terrible nature of what Elena represents lies in the fact that she is banal in the extreme in all her 'experience of life': she is 'like everybody else'.

When Oleg and I were putting the finishing touches to the script, there was one powerful image which often hovered round us and this is just the moment to recall it. The image was from *The Brothers Karamazov*, from the famous scene when Ivan is visited by the Devil. The dialogue between them is a long one but, among other things the Devil comes out with, one thought is astonishing and I would even say frightening. I shall reproduce it in my own words, but they are close to the original: "Do you know Ivan Fyodorovich, what my most cherished dream is? To assume the form of some 15-stone merchant's wife, who lights candles in church for God, and to believe everything that she believes in." The implications of this are terrible and repulsive. If the Devil's dream is to assume the form of the most ordinary of philistines, of the simplest of pagans, it follows on from this that in his far-sighted view of the world, Dostoevsky is maintaining that the face of Evil itself is to be found in the worthless and most trivial of philistines. Is that how it turns out? It turns out that this 'pernicious spirit' is spread throughout the world invisibly and so fundamentally, that it can no longer be recognised any more – in this world where true love can no longer be recognised and where only its distorted image, its simulacrum, rules human affairs and bodies. I am surprised by questions from some film-goers, who ask about the relationship between Vladimir and Elena: "Do they love each other?" Take a closer look... not at the screen, but at yourselves, What kind of blindness is that? When a person ceases to be the *purpose* for another, but is merely a *means* to an end: that leaves no room for love and cannot do so. In that situation a human being is rent in two and always remains a Smerdyakov. In order to put an end to that nightmare of split personality and to banish confusion, it is vital to choose once and for all true being, as Berdyaev[60] commented in this connection. It is imperative to tear from inside ourselves that source of putrefaction, not from inside the world altogether – a vain endeavour – but a drop at a time from inside each one of us. It is not a shared task, but one for each individual separately. As the saying goes – if you save yourself you will save the world. The Russian people have many cherished possessions and among them is the splendid proverb: "Where a peasant starts thinking, there's no trace of God!"

Question: But Vladimir is banal as well, does he represent 'evil' too?

AZ: Possibly. What is important about Elena though is that she is 'like everybody'. She looks so much like a 'simple kind woman' that she is

---

[60] Nikolai Berdyaev (1874-1948) – a Russian religious and political philosopher.

impossible to distinguish from what we consider the 'norm', some kind of 'minimal decency'. It was important to capture that elusive, most average aspect of evil – to which I have referred. Vladimir – it has to be said – is more eccentric, he is portrayed in more vivid colours.

Question: But which of those two camps – the Elena's or Vladimir's engages your sympathy more? I ask this question because it was not clear to me as a member of the audience.

AZ: I feel no sympathy for either. I am not on anyone's side. We need to be objective observers, to try and look at everything in a detached way, without pronouncing sentence or drawing moral conclusions.

Question: Is it really possible when making a film to avoid taking anyone's side?

AZ: I think so. What matters is that you should wish to find out how far you are prepared to go. The first question which I am usually asked in connection with Elena is – as I have already remarked – the question that took me by surprise about class struggle, about the confrontation between rich and poor. Journalists want to *see* this in the film. But tell me, if a film is about class struggle, what kind of message would it contain? "Kill an oligarch, break into his house"? or, alternatively, "build a higher fence and do not let the hoi polloi in"? Does anyone seriously think that one could make a film for the sake of ideas like that? Of course they involve confrontation and there is the texture of the rich/poor contrast. But that is how things have always been, and will continue to be: there are élites and the common people, which will always be oppressed even in the most communist of all possible worlds. As George Orwell said: "All animals are equal, but some animals are more equal than others." The gulf between rich and poor could be less frighteningly enormous than it is in our country today... I hope that there are no revolutionaries among us here, who believe that everything can be changed by violent means? Because the aim of this film is not to remind the audience about social differences and why revolutions take place. Even resorting to maximum violence, even exacting ultimate revenge (like Elena who in her own way 'takes revenge' on Vladimir), you will not change the world or other people or your own children and neither will you get rid of the 'rich /poor' divide. All you can change is yourself.

You have asked me to help you decide whom you should view with sympathy. I repeat once again that sympathy is not what matters here. What matters is observing yourself closely: not as if you were observing some kind of insects on screen (this one is positive and the other is not), but observing people. A human being is not merely a character, but a complex system of connections, either confused or clear, but always interesting. The tragic view for some strange reason assumes that we are capable of sympathising even with the most terrible of mortals.

Voice from the audience: I felt that there is only one character in the film who opposes the banality of evil you have been talking about and that is Katerina. She is a very interesting individual and can clearly see straight through Elena. It's a pity that so little time is devoted to her in the film.

AZ: I never measure such things by numbers of episodes, but I assumed that the main figure in the film was Elena, the second Vladimir and the third Katerina. Essentially speaking, she is part of the trio of the film's main characters. For, among other reasons, the fact that she opens up to such a degree. It's not just a question as to how many times she appears on screen. As we were completing the script I wondered whether we should focus on her space, her life, her interests. If you go on to my site, in the 'Video' section, in the chapter headed 'Episodes not included in the Film' you will find an episode with Katerina, which was duly shot but not included in the final cut of the film. It's possible that the material there will shed more light on Katerina. But not a great deal. The important things had already been said.

To be honest, I myself felt there was not enough of her. On Elena Lyadova's last day of filming (the scene with the lawyer), when we had finished, I announced "Today is Elena's final day of filming," and as is the custom on set, the whole crew applauded her. I felt really sad at that point, and thought: "How I should have liked to go on working with her."

THREE INTERVIEWS. QUESTIONS TO THE DIRECTOR

Question: We regretted it too. Katerina was the only person to grasp what Elena was up to, but she is a drug addict, an outsider, aimless and without work. One does not feel that she is capable of love. For example, when she goes up to her father's coffin, she bends down and while we can hear Elena's display of sobbing, when it comes to Katerina, we only see her face tremble a little and that is all. It's difficult to understand whether she is good or evil. Did you, as the director, ask Katerina not to cry? Perhaps, the actress was unable to?

AZ: Elena Lyadova is not someone who is 'unable' to do things. She is an actress who can do anything, believe me. We only had three or four takes and I asked her to make each new take 'wetter' than the last – that is a term used in jest. An actor might be asked to do a 'wet' take, then a 'dry' take followed by a 'damp' one – those are the gradations available.

Believe me there were 'wet' takes as well and they too were absolutely sincere and precise. In the end we chose a more controlled version, because it was more powerful. Let me repeat what I have said already with regard to Elena/Markina. I tried to achieve some sort of 'adequate expression', so that the meaning should come across with the least impact, as it were. I sought to avoid piling it on too thick or turning the whole thing into a flood of emotion, because the implications were 'coming over' without all of that. As far as I was concerned, the impact was all the stronger because a restrained person always remains something in the way of a mystery and that leads to additional overtones in the nuances of sound. During the funeral scene to which you refer, when Katerina sits down on her chair and Elena starts weeping loudly, Katerina lifts her gaze and looks at her father for the last time. That's when you see the abyss of her sadness. She has dark eyes, as black as coal – the eyes of a person lost and crushed. I feel that look has far more of an impact than any groaning.

But to continue... You say that she is a drug-addict, but that is something we only *hear* from her own lips. Why might we not think that all that is simply bravado? "Do you think that I'm a drug-addict, Papa? Has your second wife put the idea into your head, or perhaps you just like to think so? Don't you believe me? I'm tired of trying to make you change your mind!" Perhaps that's what you can read into it? It's perfectly possible. Perhaps in her youth she found it unbearable to live according to her father's materialistic values. She protested in the way she knew how, not wanting to live the way he had taught her. Perhaps that rebellious spirit had appeared at a very young age. She is, at the very least, a sincere, uncompromising, clear-sighted and honest individual. Why should we not see all that in her, for example? It's easy to stick labels on people: this one's a bad lot, that one has no chance of making it, while another has. In reality nothing's as simple as that. I think that Katerina is a character with several faces, she's a complex individual.

Question: So what's complex about her? She's a positive character, beyond any doubt!

AZ: Beyond doubt? You would be a rare member of the audience, if you are prepared to maintain that. But, in general, I think that she is not simply an empty creature living for the moment and she is definitely not someone who could not care less about anybody or anything, as Elena believes. Katerina can see that the world around her is built on lies, but she does not understand how to cope with that. She is in the same kind of state as many of us. Yet I am not in a hurry to credit her with all manner of undeniably 'positive significance'. It's not that 'good' Elena turned out to be 'bad' and 'bad' Katerina turned out to be 'good': what matters is that one woman is capable of love and the other is not. This is the most difficult and deep-rooted mystery in any individual: from outside you cannot assess her, this explains why her style of acting is restrained.

Question: If we're talking now about the restraint and semi-tones in her acting – why in Katerina's conversation with Elena do you not give her a semi-tone but let her come out with a sharp retort, when she replies to Elena's "I love Vladimir" with "Oh yes, till death do you part". I have to say, that's not what I'd call a semi-tone!

AZ: Really? I would say that she comes out with that as a very neutral expression. Or at least in a way that is completely in tune with her character. Let me tell you a bit more about that "till death do you part..." Only two people had read the script right through – Smirnov and Markina. Neither Lyadova, nor any of the others had read the whole script: each one of them only had the text of the episodes in which they appeared. You reminded me just now of that, because that phrase "Oh yes, till death do you part" could indeed have the ring about it which you assumed was there – one with real *meaning*: it doesn't sound like that though, precisely because Lyadova did not know what was happening between Vladimir and Elena or even that a murder was soon to be committed. The actress did not know the whole story and only saw it on screen on the day of the première in Cannes, when she was possibly astonished by how far-sighted her character was. It is possible that her far-sightedness makes it easier for people not to find Elena sympathetic and possibly it's just that 'it takes one to know one'. Perhaps, it's because of her love for her father...

Question: Just a small question. In the scene of the fight, lights go on along the fence. Did they come on by chance or not?

AZ: That's a good question.

Question: You mean the cameraman made a special effort?

AZ: No it's computer graphics. The power-station in Biryulovo is an off-limits building. It's difficult to get access. Even if we had managed to obtain permission to turn those lights on ourselves when we needed them, I think it would only have made our position more difficult. We were filming that episode in very tight time limits, in the short interval after the sun had set but when it was still light. It was a question of some 15 or 20 minutes. Filming the fight scene by that fence in such a short time was very difficult, because not only did it involve shooting from different positions, but also a specific number of takes. If in addition we had been constrained by having to wait for the lights on the concrete fence to be turned on, it would have taken us more than one day to complete everything.

I realised, what's more that I would not be able to do many takes. That's what made me chivvy somewhat the actor who was playing Sasha: all the time he was lying on the ground, I kept on giving him loud orders, telling him what to do. I thought that I was giving him a reliable rhythm for the scene, but later when I saw the rushes, I was horrified: everything he was doing in that shot was, one might say, hurried. At that point I realised what precisely had stopped me from making an objective assessment of the exact nature of the rhythm during the shooting – the fear that we would not have the chance to do another take. I admit that the material shocked me so much that I even thought of re-filming the episode, before I had the bright idea – you can believe me or not, as you see fit – that I could 'slow down' the action in that part of the episode.

We slowed down Sasha's movements after the fight and, moreover, in stages: sometimes by 20%, in others by 30% or even more. We did this very gently and in some places left the real speed unchanged. The result, I feel, is first-class because – for example – I myself am not aware of any slowing-down when I watch that sequence. Yet we actually slowed it down so much that it now lasts 12 seconds longer than before.

In answer to your main question about whether the lights were turned on by chance, I should like to say that things like that do not happen by chance. It is clear that we went back to real time.

Question: Forgive me for following on with another question immediately, but did you film Sasha turning his legs over after you'd shot the baby?

AZ: Splendid. You noticed the parallel and I'm very glad. No, we filmed the baby later on. First of all we did all the shots on location and only then did we come into the studio.

Question: Did that come out as it did by chance?

AZ: Yes, that comes under the heading of the 'acquisitions' we were talking about earlier. The baby was a talented lad. Just like the crow, by the way, who time and time again landed on the branch in the camera's cross-hairs.

Question: Where did the shooting take place?

AZ: It was all shot in Moscow. The two main interiors – Vladimir's flat and Sergei's – were sets that were built in the studio.

A back-drop with a photograph of the Biryulovo power station was spread outside the windows of Sergei's flat. The chimneys of the power-station had been painted in pastel colours by someone, so no effort was required on the part of our set-designer: life itself offered us those wonderful colour-schemes and shapes. The beehive-like apartment block of flats built at right-angles to those chimneys was in front of the balcony, where Sergei was smoking so pensively at the beginning of the film and it too was photographed and then transferred to a back-drop for the set.

Vladimir's flat was also set up in the studio, including the fragments of the exterior with the door opening on to the spacious balcony. Back-drops with a photograph of a Moscow courtyard came into their own for that set as well, as did the real tree trunks outside the windows and the artificial, roughly 30-kilowatt sun.

Question: Why did you decide to use a set like that rather than film in a real interior?

AZ: It's a far from simple task finding a real flat with what you need outside the windows. You probably could find something, but then arranging to film for a whole week in someone else's home is not easy. Yet in the studio we could put together the interior with anything we liked, choose the wall surface and even the lay-out of the rooms. It is in fact very convenient working in the studio, because you have everything to hand. Even the sun is always up there exactly where you need it.

Question: Tell me please about those long shots when, for example, the nurse clears up the bed-linen in the ward or the first shot in the film when the crow alights on the branch, are those long shots deliberate? What was the reason for them?

AZ: The episode with the nurse came into being, you might say, on the set itself, just a few days before it was filmed. The reason for its inclusion was as follows: it suddenly occurred to me that between the episode of Vladimir's discharge from hospital and the episode in which he informs Elena about his will, there is no time for a breather: an interlude of some kind was required. Then I had the idea about the nurse, who is tidying up the ward. Apart from that task of hers at work, there were additional implications to that scene as well. From the context of some of the remarks to be heard in the film, the audience discovers that Elena has worked in a hospital and probably in some modest capacity as a carer or, perhaps, as a nurse. She too in the past would have made patients' beds and kept an eye on their state of health: here in front of us there is a 'new Elena', or a facet of one. I should like to hope those associations would also have occurred to the audience: all that without even mentioning what I would see as the extraordinary atmosphere created precisely thanks to its particular rhythm and the long focus on the work of the nurse.

Voice from the audience: Yet you have the audience impatiently waiting for something, but nothing takes place.

AZ: So much the better – you don't need to have something happening in all the shots without exception. After all, it's not an action movie is it? I like the mood in that episode: a person is being discharged from hospital, after whom nothing remains – the sheets have been taken away, sheets which had retained his warmth, the warmth of his life... A remarkable atmosphere, I feel.

Now, as to why the first shot of the film was so long. I mentioned earlier that the rising of the sun was achieved thanks to the efforts of the lighting team in the studio. At the required moment a powerful piece of lighting equipment was raised, using an enormous stand and that created the illusion of the rising sun: warm reddish light appeared flooding across the window and then the crow flew into the shot. So from the very first frame and the first call for "Action!" till the moment when the crow settled on the branch, shook itself and straightened its feathers – that shot was being filmed for about three minutes or even more perhaps. In the film it takes one minute and twenty seconds. The ninety seconds which were not used in the film gave us the chance to observe how the shadows dispersed for a long time before the first rays of sunlight appeared.

Gradually with Anna Mass, my editor, we 'bit off' a few seconds of the shadows, while the film as a whole was taking shape. As a result of this shortening, about 45 seconds were cut. I admit that I do not find this shot long and I was prepared to watch it for a long time. The rhythm of the film as a whole, however, made us feel that the cut had to be made.

What explains the length of those shots? I think that is simply a matter of one's own sense of the rhythm of life. It is not an artificially devised narrative technique, not something that stems from some contemplative intention which can duly be explained. A texture of this kind is a matter of suggestion, it literally bewitches you and sucks you in, as if through a funnel. This makes it much easier to immerse yourself into the life on screen. Some people, by the way, find it very much of a problem and others it may simply annoy.

Question: The rhythm of your films – is that an original way of slowing down the ordinary rhythm of life?

AZ: Possibly it's some kind of subconscious reaction, a wish to create a different kind of reality similar to the actual one which lives within us, rather than the one progress forces upon us. Take a close look at someone who has been lying down for a long time after waking up and who is coming to life, just as you yourself might. At moments like that you don't watch your every move, you're just living, that's part of our make-up. Yet it is often not our own rhythm, the rhythm of our own heart, which is being forced upon us. There is even a subject of philosophical debate, which was formulated many years ago by Mikhail Epstein[61] – the way an individual lags behind mankind viewed as a fundamental law of modern history. There is so much information to hand that the individual may well come to believe that others have already read everything, seen everything and know significantly more than he does. This means he is lagging behind. He is not able to keep pace with the world. This is something with which the individual cannot reconcile himself, he moves faster, he quickens his pace. Yet that pace is only the external side of things, what is inside him is a rhythm which the eye cannot see. Pace is always visible. We can wave our hands around, 'hurl' the camera from left to right, use piles of words and endless cuts. That does not,

---

[61] Mikhail Epstein – an influential Russian culturologist.

however, create rhythm. Dynamic editing only creates pace, outward appearances.

A few years ago at the Golden Eagle Awards a film was shown in the competition for 'Best Film Editing': its makers took special pride in the fact that there were 6,000 cuts in their 90-minute film. Video-clips and brief pictures followed on from each other at a crazy pace. There are films which only have a total of 200 cuts – Tarkovsky's *The Mirror*, for instance. But in this film there were 30 times more. The old masters of the screen would use 300, 500. But here it was six thousand! Impressive, perhaps! In actual fact the end-product was a 'goulash' consisting of drops of blood, faces, clenched fists, aggressive expressions, blows and a gashed forehead.

I even had an argument with a French producer on that subject. He demanded that I should make cuts in the vignette 'Apocrypha' which was to become part of the film *New York, I love you*. The vignette lasted 8½ minutes. The whole film was put together as follows: twelve seven-minute vignettes and between them 'transitions' or fragments lasting one minute, in which some of the characters from all the longer films figured. The transitions provided the thread as it were, on which all the beads were hung. I suggested to him: "Let's use the first minute of my short – the encounter with the girl, who asks about Brodsky – as a transition?" He agreed. I thought to myself: "Fine, I've won back a minute." But there were still 7½ to do. He said: "You need to cut another 30 seconds, then your short will have the necessary rhythm." I replied: "What you call rhythm is already to be found in the material that's been shot. If I make the shots briefer still, that will not mean that the film starts to move more rapidly. The most important thing in the picture is its rhythm, which is conveyed not through initial impressions, but lives somewhere inside it and takes shape inside your very being. There's no getting round it. If I take out another 30 seconds, snipping it back in various places I shall only ruin the film. Believe me, that will not make it more dynamic. The American focus-group is still going to be convinced that it is a very slow film." Pace is an 'objective' dimension, an imaginary state of affairs... Rhythm, though, conveys what is really there, through rhythm emotions are experienced.

Question: In your film we hear the music of Philip Glass and I was interested to know whether you met him, how you worked with him? Did he write music for you or did you just buy the rights?

AZ: I don't know him. Rodnyansky wrote him a letter saying that we needed to acquire the rights so as to be able to use his music. He replied: "Why do you want my old music? Why don't I write you some new music?" That suggestion of his took the wind out of our sails. Philip Glass is a great contemporary composer. To suggest that he should write music which would be better than what he had already written seemed rather strange to us. The music which you hear in the film is the third part of his *Symphony No. 3*. It blends so seamlessly with the images that his flattering proposal to compose something new alarmed us.

The whole of the script was divided into 14 chapters. The 'Introduction', the episode that comes after it called 'Elena's Path' and later – several chapters further on – there was a fragment entitled 'Vladimir's Path' and in the final part there was 'Elena's Second Path'... I had decided in advance that music would be used in those three chapters of the film. In those chapters there were to be long 'journeys'. It seemed right to me that we should spend a long time observing Elena as she moves in the direction of her 'homeland'. A long and difficult journey. There are people who think that if you have spent 15 minutes with someone and you feel that two hours have gone by, then you should regard the process as an unnecessary torture, a waste of time: if, on the other hand, you have spent two hours with someone and have the feeling that you have only just begun to talk to them, that was worth it. Time has been compressed.

Music has a similar effect: it transforms the space in the four-minute episode 'Elena's Path' into a single minute, or even a few tens of seconds. I needed to observe Elena for a long time and Vladimir for just as long, but in order to compress that space artificially, music was required. It has been edited, it is a compilation of various elements. On the third occasion, when we are in the lawyer's office, instruments are heard for the first time, which had not been heard in the first two versions of the performance of that music. It is in actual fact a continuation of the idea of Philip Glass himself. As you know, he is a minimalist composer and minimalism specifically relies on themes being repeated and an absence of 'diversity'. Like a wheel.

Movement and monotony of movement. It was only on the fourth occasion when that music is used as background for the final credits that the theme is developed to the full.

I made a discovery for myself as early as when I saw Antonioni's *Eclipse* – the episode when the heroine Monica Vitti invites the hero Alain Delon to her place: they go into her room and the set consists of a bed, a man and a woman. There is nothing else. Then I realised that placing a woman, man and a bed in a single space is enough – tension is immediately created. There is a sense that the meaning hanging in the air is immediately going to come into its own. There are some archetypal images, which have an impact all of their own. In *Elena* nothing conveys to the audience during the first hour of the narrative that something terrible is going to happen. We simply follow the lives of these people, but for some reason at the very beginning of the film, during an insignificant episode, a feeling comes over us that seems like a foretaste of disaster. That's the effect of the music. We wrote Glass a letter expressing our gratitude, saying that the music from his symphony had been ideally suited to our purposes and that we would be happy if he would agree to work with us on our next project.

However, if I'm honest, my dream would be to make a film without any music at all, as Besson or Éric Rohmer succeeded in doing. Or the Dardenne brothers. That would be real aerobatics and so far something I have not pulled off.

Question: And tell me, when it comes to the TV... Everything you include are easily recognisable programmes. Were you intending to shed light on the inner world of the characters through the programmes they watch? If we were to say that your characters are caricatures, in that case the programmes they watch turn the film into a documentary.

AZ: The assertion that our characters are caricatures seems strange to me. As I see it, they are easily recognisable, these characters. I know these people: they sit at their tables or on their sofas like that, turn their heads and pick up objects just like that. These are my neighbours, me myself, when all's said and done. No caricatures here! As for the television, one might say that it is yet another character in the film. In our life today, everyone watches their own

THREE INTERVIEWS. QUESTIONS TO THE DIRECTOR

particular programmes: they are like a mirror reflecting the viewers. We have Elena watching 'Let them Talk'[62], Vladimir his sport and Sergei 'Six Snatches of Life'[63]. Katerina, our rebel, in an episode which is not part of the film any more, watches a documentary on the internet about the world-famous Slovenian philosopher, Slavoj Žižek, into which he throws the provocative thought: "Love is Evil".

Question: In *Elena* there is one element, which we have not yet discussed – the idea of the 'iconostasis', which hangs opposite Elena's bed, made up of her photographs. As I understand it, there is only one photograph with Vladimir, an enormous number of photos with her family, with her son and grandson, but, for example, no photograph with her previous husband, Sergei's father. But there is one of Elena in her youth. I'd like to talk about that episode...

AZ: It's surprising how closely you have studied that image. And where did you conjure up that word 'iconostasis' from? It's a surprising coincidence – that was my definition, precisely the word I used on set.

The idea came to me spontaneously really, and I would even say when shooting was in full swing: we had finished the location shots and were taking over the studio set. It seemed to me that one wall in Elena's room was rather empty. I started to think what we might hang on it, how we might liven it up, fill it up a bit and then suddenly the idea with the photographs came to me. Prior to that, immediately after we had decided on all members of the cast, we asked them to bring in photos of themselves as children and young people growing up, so that these might be displayed somewhere in the flat – either of the flats. Then suddenly I had the idea that on the wall in the bedroom opposite her bed there would be Elena's 'iconostasis'... After that there followed the idea of Elena looking at herself. Even before we started shooting that episode, I was very preoccupied with how we might enable her to look back into her past and when we put those two shots together in the editing suite – the portrait of Elena as a young girl, radiant and full of hope and the portrait of her looking

---

[62] 'Let them Talk' – a daytime TV talk show that features controversial guests and discussions.
[63] '6 Snatches of Life' – a comedy series on TV featuring low-level humour.

at herself as she is now – a spark was lit... It's like the way people in their very last moment see their whole life spread out before them and grasp with utter clarity who they really are.

Question: Tell me – am I right in understanding that there is a difference between the ways you portray the two main settings: Vladimir's flat is shown in cold tones and Sergei's in warm ones? Even the child's toy in Sergei's flat is yellowish-orange. Why do you underline that difference and is there some hidden meaning behind it?

AZ: Incidentally that yellow and orange duckling is one of my son's toys. I brought it in from home. In general, I feel, it should be clear that Sergei's interior was filmed in warm colours, in the main, and Vladimir's in cold ones. That is exclusively to contrast the alternating atmospheres, no more than that. We had not been planning to place special emphasis on the 'warm' and the 'cold'. It's a question of alternating rhythms, as I said before. There were no additional meanings or symbols to be read into it.

Question: And in general, are there any symbols in the picture?

AZ: No, none. Well which ones? Name me even one. Have you really been trained so hard to look for hidden meanings, that you approach any depiction in this way? You seem to think that there has to be some hidden, coded signal without fail and so you're concentrating all the time on how to decode it. Who taught you to do that? Leave that to the film-critics.

Question: But you created this film using the theme of the Apocalypse, so you're bound to have thought about symbols!

AZ: We rejected a language of symbols right from the start. Believe me, there isn't one.

Question: But the horse which Elena sees out of the train window? Surely that's a horse from the Horsemen of the Apocalypse? That's how many people perceived it.

AZ: I don't understand why that horse is a stumbling block for many people, why people talk about it so much.

Voice from the audience: Because it's white.

AZ: It's white because the background for it is dark asphalt and the contrast makes it stand out better. It was clear that the horse would only be in the shot for a few seconds and so we had to make sure it would be visible straightaway. That's the only reason why the horse was specifically white.

I explain this episode for myself as follows: at that stage in the film immediately after the scene in the lawyer's office, the feeling of suspense starts to fade. It's as if everything has passed, as if our worries for Elena had been blown away as she stood on the platform and now here she is travelling to her son with the 'goods', clutching the bag with the money on her lap. Everything seems to be progressing well and then suddenly... the train stops.

Voice from the audience: There's a feeling that the handbag's about to be snatched!

AZ: The handbag snatched!?... Well, anyway, the feeling of suspense returns. A squad of police passes rapidly through the carriage and in the silence of the halted train apprehension starts to grow again. We wonder whether that interruption of the journey and those militiamen have something to do with Elena's crime? All of that occurs to us because of Elena's agitated state and our own run-of-the-mill stereotypical reactions. We shouldn't forget that we (the audience) are expecting retribution.

Without us even noticing, all this begins to take effect. You see – a bag-snatch – all that is part of the idea of retribution.
Yet, if we take a broader view, you will not find a single subjective view-point in the film, everywhere there is an objective camera. It is only here, suddenly – as it seemed to me – that through that horse we were suddenly privy to Elena's inner thoughts, as if we were in tandem with her. The horse is the gateway into Elena's inner world. At least that's how the moving-off at a tangent, almost a deception, achieves its impact. The camera is then objective once more: we are

shown Elena's profile, we have a three-quarter shot of her face. There is a little girl sitting behind her, who says to her neighbour: "Look, look!" Elena also has a look and together with her we look out of the window. That is when the camera imperceptibly becomes Elena's own subjective glance.

I even remember that a member of the audience said that, when Elena looks at that horse, a shiver "went right through her". I would remind them: "From that moment when *we* saw the horse, Elena is no longer in the shot and the next time we see her is not till the entrance into Sergei's block of flats." That remark from a film-goer gives me some reason to think that the sought-after effect was achieved. In other words that viewer really did find his way into Elena's inner world: he saw everything through her eyes and could really feel what was happening to her. At least that's what I should like to think.

One thing I can say for sure. That poor wretched horse has no symbolic significance. But I like the idea of how some people see certain signs in objects, while others simply walk past.

Question: Then there's the mirror: you used one in *The Banishment*, when the heroine does her hair in front of a mirror and then here you use a mirror a second time. Why? I merely noticed that detail and it stuck in my memory. Is that some kind of sign? Is there any kind of symbol behind that image?

AZ: When a woman arranges her hair, it is simply something beautiful to look at. There's nothing more I can add.

Voice from the audience: But, nevertheless... You spoke of paying attention to signs which "want to make their way into a film" at the beginning of this discussion and just now you found yourself saying that some people walk past, while others 'see' signs in objects. I think you're not telling us the whole story...

AZ: All right then. Let me put it another way. Let's take a closer look at the concepts of 'symbol' and 'image'. It's possible that you're confusing their meanings, when you use a concept like 'sign' in this context. Without turning to Wikipedia, let's try together to feel the flavour of these things. For me personally, a Symbol is something that has been clumsily inserted into the context of a film. In my view it is wrong for the cinema to use a language like that. It is crude matter, because it can be interpreted easily. It's like calling a spade a spade or, to put it more simply still, like writing a word on a piece of cardboard to denote the object shown in the shot. A symbol in the cinema is like a transfer of literary 'knowledge': as if to say *here* this has *that* meaning. What comes over to me as the complete opposite of a Symbol is a concept like Image. What we 'write' must be of such a kind that an Image should appear in the consciousness of the perceiver and not as an object portrayed on screen. For me a Symbol is an immobile object like that. Only an Image has real power: it is not tangible, you cannot prod it with your finger, because it is present invisibly on the screen and it can only be *perceived*, but not fully explained or understood.

But when I spoke about Signs, which we can see in ordinary life, what I meant first and foremost was this. An acquaintance of mine told me about an amazing incident. He was sitting one day with his wife at a table, on which there was a large vase of lilies. The situation was atypical: it could not be said that it was usual for those particular flowers to be there in that vase. Moreover the lilies had not been placed in the vase by his wife: they just happened to be there. So he was looking at his wife and sensed that she was agitated by something and wanted to tell him something important. He looked at her, noticed this unusual bouquet next to her profile, took a closer look at it and then heard her say in a quiet voice that she was expecting a child. Someone else might not have noticed any sign in those events and circumstances, but my friend did and told me about it later. The point is that lilies are an invariable attribute of the Annunciation. In canvases of all eras portraying the Archangel Gabriel announcing to Mary that she is with child, a lily is bound to be depicted, without exception. Just now I mentioned, in passing, that the bouquet had not been placed on the table by my friend's wife and, without going into detail, we can say that the vase was standing there by chance, but the woman herself had not known about the link. Indeed, my friend himself would never have noticed the coincidence if he had not been fairly well versed in the history of art and sacred subjects. He would have been preoccupied merely with the news that his wife was announcing to him. But now, being aware of the implications of the event, he perceived the news as a sign, as a miracle. Things like that surround us on all sides, all we need to do is discern them. The cinema roams about somewhere alongside events of that kind: it seeks to capture what is miraculous, namely to create an Image.

Sensing an Image is when you succeed in filming something in such a way that something invisible begins like a mystery or a secret to lend form to the visible: it is an atmosphere around an object, the work and dramatic shaping of meanings around it. It is like splitting one and the same object in two, like 'raising' its temperature in some way. Then in your shot hair will be transformed into tresses; a face will turn into a countenance; a flower into a bloom. Meanings of their own accord will flow down the aqueduct of the drama. Alchemy has been set in motion.

Question: Where does this leave the audience? How can they discern the invisible?

AZ: Those watching the film need to make a little extra effort, to change the angle of their vision, so that hidden essences can manifest themselves through ordinary reality. Without the audience nothing is going to happen anyway. Sometimes you come across the most ridiculous statements in print about yourself: "It is in the Jarmusch tradition and there is a quotation from *The Texas Chainsaw Massacre*." I honestly have not seen the film. That was written about *The Return*. People like this see human noses and say they're pig snouts! They wrote: "Wine on the table? What the hell! Where have you ever seen wine in the Russian provinces? Peasants drink vodka!" Critics like that do not notice any other dimensions. Everything they set their eyes upon turns from shining silver into pottery shards. The world for them is nothing but a box full of pleasures. They have forgotten that wine can be the blood of Christ. Not just something to be drunk from a bottle, but a grape, fruit of the earth. Their blindness is incredible, hair-raising, primitive – but it is viewed benevolently. And what rubbish is written on the internet. It's one thing when we're talking about ordinary film-goers: they walked past, had a look and did not notice anything. But people who are professionals seriously engaged in work on meanings – journalists and critics. They appear not to notice how through their own volition they are turning into real 'robots' and 'trolls' injecting cynicism, scepticism and arrogance into the public space. The culture of the written word, of conscientious labour, of mutual trust has become over-extended and superficial. Even the academic world – this I have heard on several occasions from sensitive representatives of that milieu – is losing its spirit of throbbing vitality, of true quests and turning into a deadened and repulsively commercial enterprise. And when it comes to magazines and newspapers! The thirst for big headlines is now the most important thing: there is no time for probing beneath the surface, the key thing nowadays is entertainment. 'Highs' and 'adrenalin' are the fetishes of today. Everyone is rushing, rushing. Yet there is not the slightest urge to rush after people and explain anything. If we go back to our poor horse – it is not a 'symbol of the Apocalypse' in the sense that it does not *mean* that. That is because the Apocalypse itself can mean very different things and can be understood in different ways. The key to meaning is not a bank-card with which we obtain cash, but the treasure-house within us. Our horse only means what it let a particular member of the audience feel at that moment in the film.

Question: Yet, despite all that, you have used many quotations straight from the Bible, particularly in your first two films. There are biblical names in them and some individual phrases which refer back to the Bible. I should like to ask you, Andrey... I think I have understood the distinction between Symbol and Image and what you have been saying about sensing the invisible, the miraculous. Tell me, have you been to the Holy Land or perhaps to some other places, which gave you that feeling?

AZ: No, I have not been to the Holy Land. You and I are in it now. It's under our very feet.

We would like to express our gratitude to the cinema 'Pobeda' (Novosibirsk) for their invaluable help with the publication of this book, and also the company 'Non-Stop Production' and personally to Alexander Rodnyansky for permission to reproduce images from the film *Elena*.

***Elena*. The Making of Andrey Zvyagintsev's film**
Andrey Zvyagintsev, Oleg Negin, Mikhail Krichman

Editor *Ksenia Golubovich*
Translated from Russian by *Katharine Judelson*
Language editors *Ksenia Golubovich, Susannah Garden, Anastasija Nikitina*
Proofreader *Susannah Garden*
Designer *Elena Frolova*
Cover image *Sam Smith*
Handwriting deciphering *Anastasia Karasiova*
Print preparation of the script *Konstantin Tishenko*

Published by Cygnnet
www.cygnnet.com
IBSN 978-0-9570416-2-2

First published in Russian in 2014
ISBN 978-0-9570416-1-5

Printed by BALTO print, Lithuania
www.baltoprint.com

Distributed in the UK by Central Books
www.centralbooks.com

Copyright © Cygnnet, London, United Kingdom, 2014
Texts © Andrey Zvyagintsev, Oleg Negin, Mikhail Krichman
Translation © Katharine Judelson
Images © Non-Stop Production

All Rights Reserved. No part of this book may be reproduced or transmitted in any form or by any means, electronic or mechanical, including photocopying, recording, or by any information storage and retrieval system, without permission in writing from the publisher.